Two Wheels and a Tokoloshe

by

David Lemon

**Grosvenor House
Publishing Limited**

This book is published by
Grosvenor House Publishing Ltd
28-30 High Street, Guildford, Surrey, GU1 3HY.
www.grosvenorhousepublishing.co.uk

A CIP record for this book
is available from the British Library

ISBN 978-1-906645-51-9

Dedication

*This one is for Suzy Lee, John, Tanya
and Jonathan whose loving help kept me going
once the trip was over.
To them I must add two very fine men who
have died since I started writing this book. Kieran
Murtagh, an Irishman of Africa who left us when
he was far too young and that wonderful man
Stephen Price, whose generosity made so many
things possible. I miss you both.*

Other Books by David Lemon

Ivory Madness:	College Press, Harare 1983
Africa's Inland Sea:	Modus Press 1987
Kariba Adventure:	College Press 1988
Rhino:	Penguin Books 1989
Man Eater:	Penguin Books 1990
Hobo Rows Kariba:	African Publishing Group 1997
Killer Cat:	College Press 1998
Never Quite a Soldier:	Albida Books 2000
Never Quite a Soldier:	(South African Edition) Galago Books 2006
Blood Sweat and Lions:	Grosvenor House Publishing 2008

What They Said About

Never Quite a Soldier

'A chilling book that tells how a country fell apart.'
—*Pretoria News.*

'Lemon spins a highly readable yarn'
—*Armed Forces Journal, Johannesburg.*

'I am the richer for having read it.'
—*John Davison, South Africa.*

'I have never read such a personal, human related story.'
—*Gareth Loxton, Afghanistan.*

DAVID LEMON

'This book is one of the best I have read regarding the Rhodesian conflict.'
—Stephen Dunkley, Collector of Military Books.

'An exceptionally fine work – and there aren't too many of them around.'
—Dave Willis, Former Rhodesian Special Branch officer.

'His writing is so evocative of a world that has sadly passed.'
—Richard Clarke, Military Historian.

Blood Sweat and Lions

'An un-put-downable tribute to a man who conquered his own fears to prove that he is still full of life in his sixties.'
—Tony Ballinger, Zimbabwean Author.

David Lemon impresses with his utter honesty which makes it so easy to relate to his writing.
—Glyn Hunter, South African Author.

Brilliant wild life descriptions and compelling adventure.
—Geoff Blyth, Zimbabwean Conservationist.

Couldn't put it down. Lemon is stark staring mad but a true son of Africa.
—B.R.C. Woan, Amazon Review.

A fabulous, 'can't put it down' book – especially if you have ever despaired after reaching a 'serious' birthday.'
—Mrs A.C. Reynolds, Amazon Review.

I would have loved to have had the courage to do it.'
—Jim O Toole, Devon. UK

Author's Note

No journey such as the one described in these pages can be a totally solo enterprise. I had the fun in return for enduring a few knocks but there were many others without whose assistance, I would not have been able to start out, let alone get as far as Cape Town.

I have mentioned a few helpers in the story but a number of others have been left out – their individual contributions no less appreciated for the omission.

Lovely Jilly Wright deserves particular mention for her help and suggestions when editing the text, while my family – now scattered around the world – were of immeasurable help both during and after my journey. To you all – as well as all those others who helped in no matter how minor a capacity – I extend my heartfelt thanks.

PART ONE

The Road to Kariba

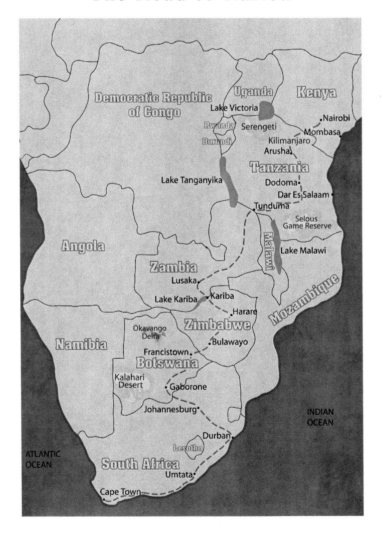

CHAPTER ONE

(A Frustrating Start)

His name was Olekwa Ncharo and red dust lay thickly on his cheeks. Flies swarmed around his face but he showed no sign of irritation. Olekwa was an Elder of the Masai tribe, which meant that although he was still a few years short of my own venerable fifty-five, he was considered too old to be a warrior and was no longer entitled to carry the heavy, long-bladed spear of the *Morani*.

Very tall and built on the lines of a stick insect, Olekwa wore an ochre-coloured blanket across his shoulders. A polished, black throwing stick dangled from his hand as he watched my labours with a vaguely quizzical expression. I was disappointed to see that he wore khaki shorts beneath the blanket but as I was to discover, East African Masailand is rapidly coming to terms with modern civilisation.

It was less than thirty six hours since I had left Nairobi and although I was still riding on tarmac, this was my second puncture. The first had occurred in the rear wheel the previous evening and I had surprised myself by the ease with which I removed and replaced the damaged tube. I hadn't ridden a bicycle for nearly forty years and the mass of chains and cogs on that wheel were pretty daunting, but the entire operation had gone extremely smoothly.

This one was in the front so I wasn't too worried as I wheeled the bike into the sparse shade of an acacia thorn and removed the panniers, before setting down to work. The sun was hot and I was sweating freely by the time I had Harriet stripped for action. It was at this juncture that Olekwa appeared on the scene and stayed to watch the fun.

I soon had the tube out, but the next step posed unforeseen problems. I carried only two spares, so repairs had to be carried out before I went on. This in itself was not a problem although I had been a mere boy when I had last repaired a puncture. As I remembered it, the procedure was not a complicated one. All I had to do was find the hole, roughen the rubber around it, apply solution and press a pre-prepared patch firmly into place. Not difficult at all – apart from the small matter of locating the actual puncture. A bowl of water was needed, I had no suitable container and besides, water was precious. This was East African Masailand where water holes are few and far between, taps non-existent. The countryside around me stretched brown and cracked into curiously liquid horizons, almost as though to emphasise the difficulties.

With both damaged tubes laid out on the ground in front of me, I pondered the problem. Carefully pouring a little precious water on to an area of rubber, I spread it around with a grimy finger. I suppose I was hoping that escaping air would betray its presence by bubbling, or at least giving some sign as it forced its way through the surface tension of the thinly spread water. That was wishful thinking. The moisture merely mingled with dust that had accumulated on the rubber, to form a muddy paste that was completely impervious to the passage of any escaping air. And this was only one small portion of the tube. Sweat ran down my face and my frustration mounted. I considered postponing repairs and moving on, but that would leave me without a spare wheel and this was very wild country. Another puncture and I would really be in trouble.

A thousand more flies drank cheerfully from the floodwaters on my face and around me, the landscape seemed to creak beneath the battering sunshine. Gritty dust worked its way into my right eye and a bird that I couldn't identify squawked in raucous derision from a nearby tree. As I wondered what to do, my lone spectator spoke to me in Masai. On his arrival, I had greeted him with 'sobbha,' (hello) the only Masai word I knew, and this had given him an entirely flattering idea of my linguistic capabilities. He spoke rapidly and it took me a while to stem the flow. In laboured Swahili, I managed to explain the situation and seemingly unphased, he switched to the more commonly used language. I gathered eventually that there was a water hole nearby to which he was happy to guide me. It seemed almost too good to be true, so draping the tubes around my shoulders and tucking the pump under one arm, I bade Olekwa 'lead on' and set off in search of water.

One thing that the traveller in Africa quickly learns is that concepts of distance are entirely relative. What to Olekwa was 'nearby' turned out to be far enough away to nearly cripple this overweight and still-very-unfit typewriter jockey. My guide covered the ground at an easy lope, seeming to spring off the balls of his feet with every step while my muscles shrieked in protest at the pace he set. Gritting my teeth, I stumbled in his wake.

After almost half an hour of hard walking, we came upon a small, scummy pool – obviously a favourite watering spot for local livestock, as the stink of urine and manure hung about the place like a pall. The water was thickly festooned with green algae, but it was sufficient for my purpose and I wasted no time in getting down to work. Once I located the puncture sites, I had to mark them with my pen, as marking chalk had not been considered in my preparations for the trip – an omission I was to regret on many more occasions.

With the punctures duly encircled in difficult-to-see, blue ink, we returned to where I had left the bike and I must confess to feeling some relief that she hadn't been touched. It was early days then and although concern for Harriet's safety had been far from my mind when we set out for the waterhole, vague worries had occurred to me while we were walking. I had started the ride with two expensive cable locks and any number of well intentioned warnings about cycle security ringing in my ears, but it usually – as on that first occasion – seemed too much of an effort and somehow insulting to those I happened to be with to use them. They remained in my pannier throughout the journey and it says much for the honesty of those I passed among that in well over seven thousand kilometres, I didn't lose a single item of kit apart from those mislaid through my own carelessness.

Still with my attentive audience of one, I repaired both damaged tubes and replaced one of them on the front wheel. For some inexplicable reason, that wheel then refused to go back into place on the bicycle. I pushed; I pulled; I tried being gentle; I tried forcing it home, but nothing worked. With sweat pouring down my face and my spectacles misting up as my blood pressure rose, I told myself to remain calm. Before I had left Nairobi, I had pasted a bumper sticker onto my rear pannier rack, which read, 'There is no Hurry in Africa.' Now I tried hard to keep that simple philosophy in mind. I didn't dare look at Olekwa, although I am sure he was too much of a gentleman to show the amusement he must have been feeling at my ineptitude.

I will never know why that wheel behaved so badly. I was to change it on many more occasions without experiencing the slightest difficulty. It was probably just that I was hot, flustered and without confidence in my own ability to effect repairs. Whatever the case, it led to a desperately frustrating ten minutes, I could well have done without.

I don't know what I did that was different, but suddenly the wheel slid easily into place and sat between its retaining arms, spinning slowly and seeming to mock my sweaty efforts. Mopping my face in relief, I hurried to tighten the nuts.

After that, the operation did not take long and I chattered to Olekwa as I worked. He suggested that I should spend the night at his village – *manyattas* the Masai call them – but I declined on the grounds that the day was still young and I had a long way to go. Once the bike was loaded, I turned to say farewell to the impassive Masai. I was thanking him for his timely assistance when he interrupted quietly.

"What about the other wheel?"

I misunderstood him completely.

"No, no – only the front one needed repair."

After all, the average Masai probably didn't see many bicycles and Olekwa might have thought I was carrying out some form of routine maintenance.

He was unimpressed and possibly a little frustrated at my naivety. Shaking his head emphatically, he gestured toward the back of the bike with his throwing stick. With an awful, premonitory feeling, I turned slowly around.

The rear tyre was completely flat.

How can one describe such a moment? For long, tense seconds the bush around us was silent. Even the birds and insects ceased their chatter as they waited for my reaction. Feeling totally demoralised, I turned back toward the watching tribesman. Helpless anger welled in my chest but I pushed the emotion away. After all, it was hardly Olekwa's fault. He had merely been pointing out my shortcomings and trying to be helpful.

"It seems you have an overnight guest after all, My Friend," I told him listlessly. "Lead on to your abode."

Once again I found myself stumbling behind the long-striding Masai. Harriet's rear wheel bumped and juddered disconsolately over the ruts while thorn scrub tore at my legs, but I didn't care. I felt depressed and not at all certain that I wanted to continue with my crazy venture. Close to seven thousand kilometres of Africa lay ahead. I was hot. I was tired and I wasn't sure that I could cope.

It was not an auspicious start to my journey.

Chapter Two

(Where Dreams Begin)

There is a main thoroughfare between Nairobi and Cape Town. It takes up six and a half thousand kilometres of the Cape to Cairo highway and in places is still known as the Great North Road.

Any traveller embarking on this road can be assured of encountering a variety of conditions. The altitude drifts between sea level and two thousand metres, the countryside from vast, dusty plains to equatorial jungle and the temperature from a baking forty degrees Celsius to below freezing in the high country. Even the road itself is a mass of contradictions. In places it is a superbly maintained, metal highway but it often degenerates into little more than a rutted bush track. In many places, the relatively modern sections of tarmac are not always as they seem. In Africa, road maintenance is usually low on the list of governmental priorities and potholes of various dimensions lie in wait for the unwary.

In 1963, Missy (who was to become my wife of twenty three years) and I accompanied her family – Mum, Dad and twin sisters Judith and Margaret – on a leisurely drive from Nairobi to Cape Town. Our transport was a comfortable station wagon and time was of minor importance. We meandered from country to country, stopping off where we felt like it and generally getting the feel of rural Africa. We had a few setbacks along the way but it was an enchanting four weeks for all of us.

Thirty-five years later, everything had changed. Missy and I were divorced and she still lived in Zimbabwe. Mum had died some years previously and the twins lived on opposite sides of the world. Margaret was nursing cancer patients in Cheltenham, while Judith had married a missionary doctor who was working in South Africa. I was struggling to churn out teenage adventure stories from a Cotswold caravan and during the bleak, winter evenings my mind often drifted back to that wonderful journey so many years ago. All too clearly, I pictured the clear skies, long dusty highways and limitless horizons of Africa. All too clearly, I remembered the laughter and love we had enjoyed together and the memories stirred my restless soul.

I longed to do the trip again but there seemed little chance of that until in nostalgic conversation, Dad Rendle mentioned that he still had the hotel invoices and receipts from our 1963 trip. Almost immediately the germ of an idea began to wriggle restlessly in my mind. I would do it again and perhaps get a book out of comparing the Africa of different eras. Even if I didn't unearth enough material for a story, I would surely refresh my soul and put some perspective back into my life. I was still struggling with the after pains of divorce and this seemed an ideal way of sorting myself out.

The major problem was transport. I had no vehicle of my own and the market state for teenage fiction seemed to preclude any chance of getting one. I did not want sponsorship, as such a trip could only be done for myself. I considered both a horse and my feet but discarded both options as impractical. It would have been great fun on a pony but veterinary regulations and modern bureaucracy would make border crossings a nightmare of red tape. Nor was I ready for a marathon walk. I have always led an active life but years behind a typewriter were taking their toll and I was both overweight and unfit.

"Why don't you take a bike?" Somebody offered one day and although I scoffed at the time, the idea stuck with me and slowly nurtured in my mind.

Why not indeed? I hadn't ridden a bicycle since my schooldays but cycling is an efficient and economical way of getting around and I didn't think even the bad roads and harsh conditions of Africa would prove much of a problem for the sturdy, multi-geared bikes produced nowadays.

But I didn't have a bicycle and soon discovered that the range of machines on offer is both vast and bewildering. There are literally thousands of different models and I had no idea what I needed. For weeks I wandered the show-rooms, admiring gleaming machinery, reading countless brochures and trying to sound knowledgeable with enthusiastic salesmen. I read extensively from local libraries and even dipped into various specialist magazines for inspiration, but be it for sport or leisure, cycling has a language of its own that is baffling to the uninitiated.

Beginning to feel confused and somewhat despondent as my prospects for adventure sank into a morass of technical data, I approached the proprietor of a small Cotswold cycle business and explained my problem. If he was in any way taken aback by my intentions, Alan hid it well. Patiently he took me through the characteristics of various sleek machines and explained their suitability or otherwise for my purpose. The prices asked for most

of these beasts were a little alarming but I eventually spotted one that I could afford if I 'went without' for a while.

Alan looked a little doubtful at my choice.

"It is a popular model," he agreed carefully, "but it is
more of a general runabout than a long distance job. It is
probably a bit heavy for what you have in mind, but…"

We studied the machine in silence as his voice tailed
away. The cycle in question was an ATB (mountain bike
to the uninitiated) with eighteen gears and a bilious colour
scheme. Overall yellow, she had crimson and psychedelic-
orange markings that were not easy on the eye. Still,
colour was not the most important aspect of my choice so
I did my best to ignore it.

Being the cycling novice that I was, I didn't see how I
could possibly need so many gears, but Alan assured me
that in the course of a long journey I would use them all
and he was right. I grew adept at flicking to a higher gear
as soon as my muscles protested and it was a pleasure to
move through the cogs and feel the speed develop as my
body coped with the lower ratio.

Thus I became the proud – if slightly doubtful – owner
of an Emmelle Cheetah, all terrain bike of hideous hue.
I christened her Harriet the Horrible for her complexion
and gradually grew to love her and look upon her as a
dear, if somewhat cantankerous friend and confidante.

After Harriet became part of my life, preparations for
my African venture began to gather momentum. Lace –
the other lady in my life – and I wandered the camping
and outdoor living centres and gathered together items
that we felt might be needed. I read voraciously on travel
in Africa although this was not always an encouraging
exercise. The travelling scribes seemed to have shared an
unending treadmill of corrupt officialdom, shortage of

necessities and unfriendly locals. Having been brought up in Zimbabwe, I was accustomed to shortages and was confident that my knowledge of African languages and custom would enable me to get along with the folk I would meet along the way.

Officialdom was another matter. Give any man a uniform and a modicum of authority when he has neither the experience nor the training for it and you have the makings of a petty tyrant. In Africa, many police and border officials have climbed the promotional ladder through criteria other than ability, while bureaucracy has curdled into a wodge of unending paperwork and red tape. This is often backed up by hair-triggered kalashnikovs and in many instances, travellers can only extricate themselves from the confusion by resorting to bribery. I have never been known for my patience or the equability of my temper, so I included one hundred U.S.dollars in notes of small denomination among my essential stores. If I had to bribe my way out of trouble then so be it. I would hand over the money and try to smile.

As preparations progressed, so my nervous doubts increased. I spent many a sleepless night wondering what I was trying to prove and to whom. My vaguely adventurous youth was a long way behind me and at my age, it was surely time I was settling down to do something with my life. Many others had already cycled far greater distances than I had in mind and I was far too long in the tooth to enjoy hardship. I had a wonderful relationship going with Lace and I was throwing it all away for the sake of – I knew not what.

Yet as the doubts multiplied, so the little imp – that African *tokoloshe* who sits on the shoulders of the restless – made his insidious presence ever more evident.

"Think of those dusty horizons," wheedled the *tokoloshe*. "Think of the bush, the wild life and the stars at night. Think of those big sunny smiles. Think of Africa."

I thought and I was lost. That *tokoloshe* knows me too well. I had to get the venture out of my system, no matter what dangers or discomforts it might entail. Once I had it behind me, I could settle down to a normal life – perhaps.

Through all my doubts, it was Lace herself who gave me most encouragement. An ingenuous lady, she recognised the need in me and although it must have pained her that I was going out of her life so abruptly, she spent long hours ensuring that my preparations were as thorough as they could possibly be. Many an evening was spent on the front step of my caravan, with me reading aloud from some well-thumbed travel tome while she sewed secret pockets, fashioned a bivvy to my specifications or compiled endless lists of the thousand and one items that might prove useful and that I would never have thought about.

Weight was a major problem. I was flying out to Nairobi with Aeroflot and the airline had assured me that Harriet would be included in my personal baggage allowance. I was allowed a mere twenty kilograms in that allowance, while my unladen bike weighed just over fourteen. Drastic paring was needed. Out went various spanners, spares and other items deemed non-essential. Warm clothing was discarded and my expensive – but heavy – front panniers were exchanged for a cheap plastic pair that frightened me with their very fragility. My final desperate measure was to wear all my clothing on to the aeroplane. Three layers tends to prove uncomfortable at the best of times but for a morning arrival at Aden where the air temperature was in excess of forty degrees Celsius, that much clothing became a pinnacle of purgatory.

In the event, I needn't have worried. Hot, bothered and harassed at Heathrow (we had broken down along the way) I went to put Harriet on the scales, only to be waved away by the young lady behind the check in desk.

"We never worry about bicycles," She told me airily. "Just put it over there and someone will collect it."

I kept my feelings to myself and wondered how I would cope without spanners.

I had given some thought to fitness preparation for the trip but being idle by nature, had postponed a beginning until it was too late. My weight on the eve of departure was eighty-eight kilograms and most of that seemed centred around my middle. I consoled myself with the thought that I would get fit as I went along and although this might not have been a logical argument, it made me feel better about doing nothing and actually worked when put into practice. Individual muscles were vociferous in their complaints over the first few weeks of the trip, but as the days ground by, so my fitness increased and cycling vast distances became very much a matter of course.

But that was in the future and almost without realising it had happened, I found myself approaching the Customs desk at Jomo Kenyatta airport in Nairobi. Harriet the horrible - her tyres flat, her pedals removed and her handlebars reversed for the flight – wobbled precariously on a trolley in front of me and my heart hammered with a nervousness that had built up steadily throughout the twenty-six hour journey.

Even without the horror stories I had read, the Kenyan High Commission in London had been anything but encouraging. They insisted that my bike would not be allowed into the country without a *carnet de passage,* which turned out to be a form of insurance cover, issued by the motoring organisations. The AA had laughed at my request, while the RAC had quoted a price exactly double the amount I had paid for the bike so I had resolved to take my chances on arrival. As I pushed the cumbersome trolley through Nairobi Airport, I wished I had been more conscientious.

A jaundiced-looking customs officer watched my approach without interest. After a moment of silence while I stood humbly before him, he jerked his chin at the teetering bicycle.

"What are you going to do with that?" He invested the pronoun with considerable disdain.

"I am going to ride it to Cape Town." I told him and it sounded ridiculous, even to me.

The official looked me up and down very carefully before speaking. No doubt he was taking in my rumpled appearance, sparse grey hair and definitely middle-aged figure while pondering on the infinite folly of Mankind.

"*Mzee,*" he said at last, using the respectful term of address reserved for the elderly. "Africa is full of fools on bicycles but they are all young fools. Why don't you leave such idiocies to them? At your age, it is time to sit in the sun, shout at your wives and drink beer."

Over the ensuing weeks I would almost become accustomed to being addressed as 'Old Man' in a variety of languages but on that initial occasion, it was positively hurtful. I covered my dismay by laughing and the officer shook his head in sorrow. For a moment, I didn't realise that he had stamped my passport and was pushing it back towards me.

"Go well *Mzee*," he said sadly. "I hope you arrive safely at your destination but I fear I will be reading of your death or disappearance before too long. There is nothing worse in this world than an old fool."

I was too elated at getting through this first hurdle to worry about his words, but I remembered them later and they did little for my confidence.

Thanking him profusely, I grabbed my passport and was out of that hall with Harriet before he could change his mind. I felt quite euphoric with relief. Harriet and I were officially in Kenya and my bribe float was still intact. Adventure in the sunshine lay ahead and I was grinning all over my face as I emerged into the arrivals hall.

<hr />

Kieran Murtagh was an old friend of mine and his lovely lady, Zoe Harding had been a fount of helpful information in the weeks leading up to my departure. They were in the crowd awaiting the arrival of my flight and although Kieran greeted me with the gentle Irish smile I remembered so well, Zoe immediately dampened my elation.

"Does that thing fold up?" She enquired, indicating Harriet and sounding as doubtful as had the Customs chappie. It was the first time Zoe had actually met me and I could see that my somewhat fuller than usual figure did not exactly fill her with confidence. I admitted that 'that thing' didn't.

"We'll never get it into the car," she said and it was a difficulty that had occurred to me but been submerged beneath the weight of subsequent problems. After some discussion, it was agreed that Zoe and Kieran would take my kit and I would ride the fifteen kilometres into Nairobi. It was hardly what I needed after a long and uncomfortable flight via Moscow, Cyprus and Aden, but there was no alternative so I made the best of it. Divested of my superfluous clothing and happy to feel the sun on my legs once more, I soon had Harriet reassembled and ready for the road.

It was while I was leaning over the crossbar to tighten the last pedal nut that I heard the whispered passage of a bird overhead and felt a squidgy thump as something landed squarely in the centre of my bald patch. A gingerly exploring hand told me that the bird had deposited its calling card with deadly accuracy and I grimaced as my palm came away all sticky and wet. Zoe noticed my discomfiture and grinned.

"It is a sign of good luck," she told me impishly. "Welcome back to Africa."

Moments later the three of us had collapsed in helpless laughter. My welcome home might have been a trifle unorthodox but it was certainly a warm one. That night I wrote in my journal,

6th June

'It feels so marvellous to be back in Africa. Quite apart from the sunshine, it is the smells that make me feel at home. The smell of dust and hot dry grass, the stench of a dead dog at the roadside: the city smell of drains as I came into Nairobi itself and the smell of spices, curry powder, exhaust fumes and traditional beer as I meandered through the suburbs. Adventure beckons from all sides and it feels good to be home.'

CHAPTER THREE

(The Open Road)

Of all the African cities I passed through on my journey, Nairobi was the most impressive. I had finished my schooling there in 1961 and when Zoe and Kieran took me sightseeing, I couldn't get over the changes that had taken place in this city of my youth. The sleepy, colonial town of the early sixties had become a bustling, vibrant metropolis. People were friendly, the shops well stocked and the restaurants excellent. If the traffic was a little frightening – well it is much the same in all large cities nowadays.

One not-so-pleasant aspect of the place was the state of the roads. Riding through the suburbs one afternoon, I was appalled at the number and size of the potholes and Zoe muttered darkly that they were far worse 'out of town.' I laughed off her warnings but perhaps I should have paid more attention, as both potholes and corrugations would cause me major problems over the weeks ahead.

I spent seven days in Nairobi and it was with considerable regret that I said my farewells to Zoe and Kieran and found myself cycling out of town early one Thursday morning. I had enjoyed the week with my friends, but now I had something over six and a half thousand kilometres ahead of me and it was a daunting prospect. My stomach was sore with anxiety but whether this was due to the prospect of imminent adventure, the dangers involved or the distance I had to cover, I wasn't sure.

The city streets were still dark when I left and Harriet didn't carry a light, but I had no trouble with early morning traffic. Motorists gave my wobbling progress a wide berth and at one roundabout, a white-sleeved traffic policeman eyed my over-laden bike with evident curiosity when I pulled up beside him. When I told him where I was going, he roared with laughter and stopped the traffic in all directions. Wishing me 'very good luck, Sah' and shaking his head at the foolishness of foreigners, he waved me through and I felt many curious eyes on my back as I cycled self-consciously onward.

The Tanzanian border at Namanga was only two hundred kilometres from Nairobi on a flat road, so this was a fairly easy start to my journey. I made excellent progress and crossed into Tanzania on Saturday morning, feeling really pleased with myself, although the first step had not been without its moments of trauma.

I had my first puncture on Thursday evening and after changing the damaged tube for a new one, I was in buoyant mood. A cup of celebratory tea seemed called for but a thorough search of my kit revealed that I had left my cooking utensils in Nairobi. Having retired for the night, tealess and irritable, my sleep was disturbed by someone or something prowling around the perimeters of my camp. I was unable to identify the intruder because my new and very expensive hunter lantern would not work. I later discovered that the switch was loose and my heavy-duty batteries had spent their entire lives illuminating the inside of a pannier. I was eventually able to buy both batteries and an enamel mug at a wayside *duka* and the mug turned out to be probably my best purchase of the entire trip. It did duty as my kitchen and my bathroom. In it, I boiled water, cooked food and cleaned my teeth. On odd occasions it acted as laundry for socks or handkerchiefs and it came in handy as a roadside shower on particularly hot days. The mug soon lost its bright blue colour but it came to be a talisman of sorts. Before moving out of camp in the mornings, my last check was always for my mug, resting blackened and gungey on top of my bedroll.

For all the minor dramas involved, that initial stretch to Namanga was a wonderful reintroduction to Africa. Almost as soon as I left the outskirts of Nairobi, the Kenya plains stretched away around me, distant horizons melting into the warm blue of that vast sky. Lazy giraffe regarded me with evident curiosity and I saw ostrich, wildebeest, zebra, kongoni and gazelle in those first two days. The people I met along the road were friendly and curious as to my motives for cycling through their country. If they shared the opinion of the airport Customs officer, they were far too polite to say so and storekeepers pressed fruit and *mandazis* on me, seeming a little put out when I insisted on paying. *Mandazis* are strange little batter balls that are dipped in sugar and deep-fried. A staple throughout East Africa, they are delicious and brim full of energy so I munched on them whenever I could, all the way through Kenya and Tanzania.

On the second afternoon out from Nairobi, the weather became very hot, I had my second and third punctures and ended up as a house guest of Olekwa Ncharo.

Like most dreamers, I have often envied the lifestyle of the Masai and other nomads. They build their simple villages, graze their livestock around them then move on once the grazing is finished. It all seemed so very romantic, but then I had never been a guest in a Masai *manyatta*.

When we arrived, Olekwa's family crowded around us and plied us both with questions. I left Olekwa to do the explaining while I looked around me in eager fascination.

The *manyatta* covered an area of about two hundred square metres and was enclosed by a tightly-meshed *boma,* made from *acacia mellifera* branches, piled haphazardly together. *Mellifera* is one of the shortest of the *acacia* trees and has small, but effectively hooked thorns that made a frightening barrier for any predator. Within this tiny enclosure were four dwelling huts as well as rude pens for cattle and goats. Unlike most such villages in Africa, little attempt had been made to sweep the area and flies and discarded litter were everywhere.

I was introduced to the family and their smiles were bright and inquisitive. Including Olekwa, there were fifteen family members on view. One very old couple who must have been grandparents, two other men of Olekwa's vintage and four women of the same general era. There were also three runny-nosed toddlers, a twelve year old wearing a strange, elliptical headdress and a couple of elegant *morani* who carried the long battle spears of serving warriors. Their hair was built up with red mud and braided into elaborate coiffures, while as far as I could see, they wore no shorts beneath their *shukas*.

These two dandies and the youngster with the 'bonnet' evinced particular interest in my journey and I answered their excited questioning as well as I could. My Swahili had been good as a teenager and it was improving with usage. I even managed a few questions of my own.

The strange headdress was made from grass plaited over a wire frame and turned out to be a circumcision bonnet, to be worn by the youngster until the operation was carried out. It looked terribly uncomfortable but obviously gave him a certain standing in family circles and he didn't seem to mind.

When in answer to a question, I mentioned that I was heading for Cape Town they showed no particular surprise. The taller *moran* nodded gravely and asked in conversational tones.

"Will you get there today or tomorrow?"

I thought he was pulling my leg at first, but a glance at his face showed that the question had been a serious one. He had not the faintest idea where Cape Town might be and when I gravely told him that it could take a little longer, he seemed bemused by my tardiness.

Olekwa himself had disappeared soon after our arrival and didn't return until well after dark. By then, other problems had arisen.

The first of these was the avarice of the Masai themselves. These, the 'Noble Savages' of Hemingway and Ruark have long since fallen under the spell of the almighty dollar. Encouraged by increasing numbers of thoughtless tourists, they have come to realise that they are an extremely marketable commodity and are always keen to exploit their commercial value. I knew nothing of this however and when it was cunningly suggested that I might care to photograph my surroundings, I was quick to reach for my camera, only to be completely taken aback when one of the dandified warriors demanded two hundred shillings before I began.

"What for?" I asked in genuine innocence.

"To take *pichas*," he told me, gesturing expansively at the scruffy enclosure and his assembled family, all of whom had adopted what they must have felt were suitably photogenic poses for the occasion.

I had no intention of haggling for the privilege of photographing this motley bunch so regretfully repacked my kit. In no way abashed by the failure of the deal, my hosts chattered on as though nothing had happened.

I was to encounter many more instances of this mercenary streak over succeeding weeks. It wasn't confined to the Masai either. Most folk in East Africa were friendly and helpful but there were many who would only lend a hand for payment in advance. Even the children got in on the act. These little monsters would run from their kraals with shrill shouts of '*mzungu, mzungu*' (white man, white man) at my approach but their interest was purely pecuniary. They would follow me for kilometres, their little hands outstretched while they piped out their entire English vocabulary – 'give me money.' Occasionally the demand was accompanied by heart rending pantomimes of starvation, usually performed by the fattest and healthiest looking of the *mtotos*. I tend to get annoyed very quickly by this sort of emotional blackmail and one or two of the supplicants might well have added a few examples of choice Anglo Saxon profanity to their verbal repertoire after my passing.

The next problem to arise in the *manyatta* – a purely personal one this time – was the accommodation offered for my comfort. I have never been fastidious about where I sleep and have enjoyed many a restful night in places that the average person might regard as far from comfortable, yet I would hesitate to recommend the amenities of a Masai home to my worst enemy.

The oval-shaped sleeping huts are built from a mixture of mud and cow dung, spread over a sapling framework and baked by the sun into an impermeable crust. Each hut is a little less than two metres long and a metre high, with a tiny oval doorway set at right angles to the line of the building. There are no windows and the only ventilation comes from tiny slits set into the top of the hut. It all sounds quite cosy but this form of construction allows neither light nor air in and nothing at all out.

After a strangely sustaining supper of curdled milk mixed with blood drawn from the neck of a resident cow, I made a cautious entry into the hut, pointed out as mine for the night and felt myself recoil from the stench that met me from within. It was compounded of stale dung, urine (presumably human as there are no toilets in Masailand) wood smoke and unwashed bodies. The darkness was absolute and I was expected to share this luxury with the *morani* and the circumcision novitiate. I lasted only minutes in the foetid gloom before deciding that the cattle pen offered more chance of restful repose.

So I moved my sleeping bag outside once more, breathing in lungfuls of clean(ish) air as I emerged from my dungeon. My companions seemed a little surprised at my decision to move out but obviously didn't mind as it gave them more room. The livestock were not as enthusiastic. They were disturbed by the activity and by my presence among them and kept stamping and moaning so that I still found it impossible to sleep. Eventually I picked my way out through the *boma* and settled down in long grass, thankfully looking up at the great, gleaming bowl of the sky, the stars cold and pristine against the deep indigo backdrop.

Thus ended my second day and even if a few illusions were shattered and I spent the night with an aftertaste of smokily bitter blood and milk in my throat, I was pleased that I'd had the opportunity to observe one of Africa's glamour tribes at close quarters. Never again will talk of these idle, opportunistic nomads evoke nostalgia in my breast. I will remember only their avaristic lust for money and the degradation of their living conditions. Yet my night among the Masai was one that will live on in my storeroom of memories and my only regret is that I have no photographs to enhance that memory.

I won't forget the taste of blood and milk in a hurry either.

CHAPTER FOUR

(Trauma in Tanzania)

Tanzania is a vast, bewildering country and although I found it extremely interesting in its variety, it provided me with more troubles, traumas and shocks to my system than any other section of my trip. I was arrested twice – a new experience for a former copper – beaten up by armed soldiery, smashed a front wheel in a pothole and went down with amoebic dysentery. I also suffered extremes of thirst and fatigue in the mountains and met some truly fascinating people.

Arusha was the first major stop on my journey and it gave me the chance to rest tired muscles, clean up my kit and reflect on the few hundred kilometres that lay behind me.

From a physical point of view, the first few days had been enormously taxing but my body was toughening up and the initial aches and pains were diminishing. I had grown accustomed to sleeping on the ground once more and indeed, looked forward to nights spent in the bush with only the immensity of the night sky above me and the sounds and smells of wild Africa surrounding my resting place.

In spite of considerable apprehension on my part, the border crossing at Namanga had been without incident. The official who stamped my papers hardly glanced at me and didn't enquire as to how I was travelling. He seemed uninterested in my inoculations or what foreign currency I was carrying. A *carnet de passage* wasn't mentioned, but I am not sure whether he even knew I was travelling by bike. I certainly wasn't about to volunteer the information. The roll of black market shillings, I had hastily stowed into one sock felt uncomfortable and horribly obvious as I limped out of the building, but the discomfort was soon forgotten in my euphoria at finding myself back on the road without having been arrested or given a hard time by the authorities. I sang raucous songs of Scotland as I pedalled gently through the vast dusty plains of Tanzanian Masailand and all was well with my world. I might have been alone in the entire universe, although at one point, a solitary goat looked up at my passing before going back to bewhiskered foraging in the grass beside the road. He had obviously seen overloaded cyclists before.

On my first afternoon inside the country, I stopped to refill my water bottles at a road block outside Longido police post. There was a bored looking constable sitting under a tree and picking his teeth so I approached him to ask where I could get some water. With a jerk of his chin and without pausing in his dental endeavours, he directed me into the little building where I was a mute witness to instant justice – Tanzanian style.

A youngster of about eleven years old was stretched out across a table while a grizzled police sergeant laid into his bottom with a stout branch. The proceedings were enthusiastically presided over by a buxom, well dressed matron who – a little smugly perhaps – informed me that the youth had been caught stealing from her shop.

"This way is better than Court," she assured me. "It is less bother for everyone and he won't do it again."

The youngster's anguished howls and the clouds of dust flying from the seat of his pants at every stroke of the lustily wielded branch certainly added weight to her pronouncement. I winced with each flat thud of connection, but once back on the road and reflecting on the incident, I couldn't help feeling that perhaps the good lady had a point. Bush justice might seem somewhat barbaric to the western mind, but I too doubted whether that young fellow would ever re offend – which is surely what punishment ought to be about.

Forty-eight hours in this vast, empty slice of Africa increased my feeling of well-being and I arrived in Arusha, dusty, tired and contented. Feeling the need for comfort after the rigours of Masailand, I booked in to the Arusha Tourist Inn – a square building of faded grandeur - where the receptionist, a lovely lad called Robert Mbize expressed horror when I queried the security of my bicycle.

"Tanzanians are the most honest people in the whole world," Robert assured me earnestly. "Everything you have is safe while you are in our wonderful country."

He was right too, but such faith in one's compatriots seemed singularly inappropriate when I counted the padlocks on the front of a local electrical emporium. There were fifty-eight – ten of them on the heavy steel door itself. The shop assistants must have racked up hours of overtime merely opening up for the day.

After sleeping in the bush and rising with the morning star for the past week or so, I might have expected a couple of lovely, lazy lie-ins once I had arrived in civilisation, but that was not to be. My hotel was in that part of town where Muslims gather to pray and before first light each morning, the wailing tones of the *muezzin* from three different mosques brought me scrambling, wide awake from my bed. It was not the ideal start to my day.

But I was well rested when I headed south from Arusha and a wide, excellently maintained highway had my legs pumping easily and the bike speeding along. For the first time, I heard Harriet sing – a high-pitched, thrumming sound that came from her tyres on the tarmac and added impetus to my peddling. It was an exhilarating morning and the kilometres seemed to fly past throughout that day. I waved cheerily to passers by and returned their salutations of *'shikamoo'* with the proper response – a gravely uttered *'mahraba.'*

Although it comes from Swahili, the *lingua franca* of East Africa this greeting is peculiarly Tanzanian. *Shikamoo* is a contraction of *'shika moyo yangu,'* which means 'take hold of my heart.' The reply is a simple 'certainly if that is what you wish' and I was very pleased with myself for having found this out for myself. I even ventured the odd *shikamoo* of my own on occasion and it invariably earned me a shy smile and an enthusiastic greeting in return.

It was late afternoon when I pulled in at the Minjingu guesthouse for a rest and a cool drink to restore strength to flagging muscles. In the bar I met Eleuter Kigahe, a game ranger from the nearby Tarangarire national park. He came over for a chat and shook his head on learning that I intended to cycle all the way to Cape Town. Unlike the Masai, Eleuter certainly knew where it was.

"English people are all mad," he told me seriously. "You come to Africa and you walk or take buses all over the country. You Sir are madder than most because you ride a bicycle. How can you expect to go so far? Cape Town is a very long way to ride."

As gently as I could, I explained to Eleuter Kigahe that not only was I perfectly sane but I was not English. Coming from Zimbabwe, I was as African as he was. He was not having that.

"You are English," he insisted. "You are not African."

"I am Zimbabwean," I countered. "Therefore I am African."

We argued genially about my ancestry and the colour of my skin, eventually agreeing that neither was a complete bar to my being African. Temporarily baffled, Eleuter drank deeply of his beer then hit upon a clincher.

"How old are you?" He asked abruptly.

"Fifty five."

"How many children do you have?"

"Three."

A wide grin split his features and the light of triumph gleamed in his eye.

"Therefore you cannot be African," he pronounced with absolute conviction. "If you were, you would have fathered many more children. I myself am only forty five and already I have nine."

He glanced around for support and dragged across a round-faced character, I had already placed as the proprietor.

"Tell my cycling friend here how old you are," he commanded.

"I am just forty," the man admitted.

"How many children do you have?"

The round face looked vaguely sheepish.

"Ten."

The game ranger turned on me in triumph.

"There you are. We are true Africans, not because our skin is black but because we provide for our future with children. You white people are rich so you don't worry about old age. Our children are to help us through the later years. Without many children, you cannot be African."

With that argument successfully concluded, he turned to other matters.

"Where will you sleep tonight?"

I shrugged. There were two hours of daylight left and I hadn't given the matter much thought.

"You will have to stay here."

Eleuter had obviously appointed himself my mentor and I wasn't sure whether this was because he had bested me in argument or just that he felt he owed the proprietor a favour for contributing toward the victory. For the next half hour he regaled me with lurid tales of travellers who had fallen foul of wild animals in the area. I didn't believe a word of them but it seemed easier to agree and stay put for the night. It was a serious error of judgement on my part.

Perhaps the kindest way to describe the Minjingu guesthouse is to call it a fleapit. The rooms were basic in the extreme and the communal toilets were an hygienist's nightmare. I managed an unsatisfactory wash in a bucket of murky water cajoled from the management, but was chary about taking advantage of any other facilities on offer. One of these was brought to my attention long after I had retired for the night.

With Harriet sleeping beside me, I was almost comfortable on a bed without a mattress and fortunately had locked the door for once. Gently fading into sleep, I became instantly awake at the sound of whispering in the corridor outside my room. I had no wish to become a Tanzanian crime statistic and as a lone traveller I was extremely vulnerable.

I listened intently, but this conversation was punctuated by girlish giggles and I was not overly surprised to hear a gentle knock on my door. When I didn't reply, the handle was tried so I called out.

"Who is it?"

"Christina Sir; we wish to speak with you."

I wasn't sure who the 'we' might be but I had noticed Christina earlier in the evening. Ostensibly a waitress, her garishly painted face and the way an ample bosom struggled to escape from her entire ensemble of a dirty petticoat, made her more usual occupation readily apparent. From the lustful leers that followed her progress around the bar, I didn't think she lacked for customers but perhaps like Eleuter, she thought I was rich. If so, she was going to be disappointed.

"Go away," I shouted. "I am tired."

More knocks and giggles followed at regular intervals but eventually they left me alone and I am sure that the story of the peddling *mzungu* who didn't fancy Christina provided a topic of ribald amusement in the bar for the rest of the evening. It would certainly have convinced the clientele that whatever my claims, I could not possibly be African.

That night did eventually pass but there were times when I wondered if it would ever end. Mosquitoes were out in force and I itched constantly, although this had little to do with the depredations of *anopheles*. Nasty red blotches on my body the following morning showed that my mattress had been home to far more than one travelling cyclist.

It is hardly a place I remember with affection, but the bed bugs of Minjingu – and Christina of course – will ensure that it is a place I will not forget.

⟨✦⟩

There were other nights in Tanzania when my sleep was disturbed for one reason or another but perhaps the most frightening and potentially disastrous one occurred when I slept in a long-neglected maize field, thirty kilometres north of Dodoma.

I had crawled into the field shortly after dark and settled down for what I hoped would be a comfortable night. Softly rotten stalks provided an excellent mattress and the stars were out in force. I looked forward to a bath and good meal the following day and fell asleep, extremely content with my lot.

I awoke after midnight to a cacophonic avalanche of sound. There were crashing explosions, the terrifying whistle of mortar bombs and the crackling rattle of automatic fire. Tracer arced over the spot where I lay and the whole scenario brought back horrific memories of the Rhodesian bush war.

Scrambling from my sleeping bag, I peered into the darkness. Vivid orange flashes lit up the scene but I couldn't make out what was happening. Dodoma was the administrative capital of Tanzania at the time, so it surely had to be a coup. The implications were not pleasant. As a white foreigner, I would be an obvious target for both sides and would not be the first lone traveller in Africa to simply disappear and not be seen again. Wrapping my sleeping bag loosely around me, I wondered what to do.

After forty minutes or so, the sounds of warfare began to diminish and then ceased abruptly. My immediate instinct was to get on my bike and pedal for distant horizons as fast as I possibly could, but a little reflection told me that such a course of action would be foolish. I had to find out what was going on and which faction in the conflict would look on me more favourably than the other. Daylight would clarify the situation and I had to sit it out. If the worst came to the worst, I would have to turn back. That thought did not appeal. The prospect of recrossing three gigantic mountain ranges that had already come close to bursting my heart and ripping my overtaxed muscles to shreds was not a nice one. I had to go on. I was not going to turn back. When the alternative is as forbidding as those horrific mountain climbs, it is easy to be brave.

My reverie was broken by the sound of a heavy vehicle moving slowly along the main road. It was running on sidelights and I watched in horrified fascination. I don't suppose I was particularly surprised when it halted at the very spot where I had left the road so very long ago. The truck was forty metres from me and effectively cut off any prospects there might have been for making a clandestine exit from the scene. To make matters worse, I heard voices and movement from the opposite direction and I was suddenly very scared. In the fitful moonlight, I watched a party of armed men heading directly toward the spot where I crouched so abjectly and my heart hammered in mounting panic. Huddling further into the illusory cover of my sleeping bag, I wondered how to explain myself when they found me. The consequences were too awful to contemplate I was a white man – a foreigner – obviously hiding in the bush. I was dressed in a green bush shirt and carried camera, tape recorder and various notebooks. My story of cycling through Africa seemed suddenly improbable, even to me. Holding my breath, I was distinctly aware of the way my heart hammered against the inside of my chest. To be brutally honest, I was scared stiff.

By enormous good fortune, the soldiers were using a path that ran parallel to the one on which I crouched, but they still passed within ten metres of me. There were almost two dozen men in the party and they were all armed, their rifles slung casually across their shoulders. They moved in total silence and how they missed spotting Harriet and I in the moonlight, I shall never know. I can only assume that they were tired and eager to get into their beds.

Hiding my pale face as they moved on into the darkness, I listened to the sound of their muffled voices as they boarded the waiting vehicle. Wet through from an accumulation of sweat and dew, I was trembling with reaction and close to complete panic. Even when the lorry moved off, I still expected to be seen and summarily arrested.

Further sleep was impossible, even though the rest of the night passed without incident. As soon as a sliver of daylight appeared on the horizon, I was up, packed and ready to move. In my haste to depart, I managed to mislay my spectacles and after a frantic search, found them dangling from my neck by their retaining cord.

I've always tried to be cool, calm and collected in any crisis, but this was one occasion when my nerves got the better of me and I ended up as a dithering wreck..

Moving cautiously back on to the road, my already overtaxed heart nearly stopped when I came face to face with three soldiers taking an early morning constitutional. They were all armed but didn't appear to have any purpose in mind so I greeted them as cheerfully as I could in the circumstances. They returned my saluta-tions with somewhat puzzled expressions and then I was aboard and pedalling hard, expecting to hear them shout or feel the crashing impact of a bullet in my back at any moment.

Nothing happened and I had covered almost two kilo-metres when I came upon an explanation for the events of the night. On the edge of the road stood a sign advis-ing the world in large black letters that this was a military training area, entrance was strictly forbidden and anyone taking photographs was liable to prosecution.

I had obviously tried to sleep through a night exer-cise, carried out by the army and that sign brought the implications of my folly home with ever more vivid em-phasis. I really had been incredibly lucky. Had those re-turning soldiers spotted me in the grass, I would almost certainly have been taken for a spy and ended up qual-ifying for a long service award in some awful Tanzan-ian prison. I didn't suppose they had heard of Amnesty International or basic human rights in so remote a cor-ner of Tanzania.

A little further along the road I passed the Mukuturoa military barracks and received another shock to my system when I was hailed by an efficient looking officer. He was unarmed but carried a leather-covered cane and exuded an air of confident authority that terrified me. He was only interested in my travels however and we chatted amiably before parting with a handshake. I was heartily thankful that he hadn't asked me where I had spent the night.

Most of my nights in Tanzania were not as dramatic. Hotels were so reasonably priced that I took advantage of their services wherever I could. I stayed in many of the establishments we had used in the sixties and was amused and reassured to find that many of the railway hotels kept up an atmosphere of faded colonialism. In Mbeya this even went as far as having solid silver sugar bowls in the centre of each dining table. The bowls were stamped with the logo of the old East African Railways and Harbours and must have been worth a small fortune. Presumably they had sat elegantly undisturbed throughout the forty years or more since the E.A.R.& H. had been dissolved. With a wry smile I reflected that perhaps Robert Mbize had been right about the innate honesty of his compatriots.

The only problem with staying in hotels was a purely personal one. Eating in the dining rooms made me feel incredibly lonely. On the 1963 trip, I had been in the same dining rooms but as part of a six-strong party and mealtimes were enlivened by family chatter. Now I was totally alone and ate in silence. I ate alone in the bush too but that never worried me. On the road, I was alone but never lonely, while in hotels, I was surrounded by people and felt totally isolated. None of it made sense.

In Iringa I stayed at an excellent Indian-run hotel but undoubtedly the best value for money I encountered was at the Conference Centre in Babati.

Situated in thickly wooded hills, two hundred kilometres south of Arusha, Babati was a typically colourful, Tanzanian metropolis. Flimsy shacks made from cardboard or corrugated iron sheeting nestled for comfort against fine modern buildings and the smell of muddy decay permeated the atmosphere. The buildings and their ramshackle neighbours provided further stark contrast with traditional mud huts and temporary dwellings made from plastic sheeting, laid over twisted poles. The entire town was an incredible miscellany of architectural variety and extremes.

Ragged children played among the buildings while scrawny dogs skulked through narrow alleyways, their ribs sharply defined beneath matted, scabby skin. Heavily-laden donkeys moved listlessly toward the commercial centre of town where Indian-run *dukas* displayed the usual assortment of bicycles, dress material and cheap blue soap. Tailors pedalled their antique Singers on open verandas while on every street corner, vendors exhorted uninterested passers by to sample their personal lines in sticky sweetmeats and fiendishly tasty *samosas*. Babati was mentioned by Hemingway in at least one of his books about hunting in Africa. In his day, the place consisted of an Indian *duka* and a couple of small, wayside bars that catered for thirsty hunting parties on their way to the Serengeti plains or other remote areas. Safari parties would swap notes as they passed each other and a good time was had by all. When I arrived in town one sultry afternoon so many years later, I was disappointed to discover yet another urban centre where the air was filled with the strident din of amplified music and assorted bicycle bells. A few years prior to my visit, Babati had experienced particularly heavy rains and as nobody had thought to clean out the drains in decades, the town was flooded and many of the larger buildings were washed away. A Scandinavian aid agency stepped in with a rescue operation, but from the look of the town centre, another heavy rainstorm would lead to the same result. The roads were rutted and litter lay knee deep on the corners. The inhabitants greeted me warmly enough however, and I was directed to the Conference Centre as an ideal place to spend the night.

It was too. For a modest three hundred shillings (£1 at the time) I had a comfortable room, the use of a communal shower with hot water, dinner and even breakfast if I needed it. Astonishing value by any standards, but even more so when I considered that the tribulations of Minjingu (even without the dubious benefits of Christina's services) had set me back over a hundred shillings more than that.

It was in Babati that I met up with Freddy K. Matunga. I was enjoying an evening pipe on a bench beneath a giant acacia tree when he strolled across to join me. He was obviously a fellow guest and we sat in companionable silence for a while, each of us lost in his own thoughts. Mine were mainly concerned with the peaceful, peculiarly African ambience of my surroundings. In places like Babati, the frenetic bustle of modern life grinds itself into despair against the timelessness of Africa and I doubt that it will ever change. I smiled as a bus thundered into the main street, only to have its hurtling passage halted by the leisurely progress of an old man with a donkey-drawn scotch cart. The bus hooter blared fruitlessly into the evening air and nearby chickens cackled in indignant protest. With much excited revving of the engine, the bus driver managed to edge his vehicle around the seemingly oblivious geriatric, only to have his progress thwarted once more by two youngsters driving their cattle home from the grazing lands. The beasts swung their heads to gaze somnolently at the frustrated driver and my grin grew wider as I imagined his explosive comments.

There was a football game in progress somewhere nearby and I could hear the occasional blast of the referee's whistle and sporadic clapping from the spectators. The rapidly cooling air was clear and I savoured the gentle redolence of hot dust, dry grass, assorted livestock and giant acacia trees that is the very essence of an African evening. Smoke from my pipe drifted gently around my head and I felt very much at peace with myself and the world.

As is the way with such encounters, my companion and I began to chat – desultorily at first and then with more animation as we warmed to a theme – on this occasion, the situation in modern Tanzania.

Freddy K. Matunga (that was how he introduced himself) was a senior magistrate and was in Babati on official business.

"The court here is in a terrible state," he told me sadly. "The local police are both inefficient and corrupt, with the result that nothing gets done. Petty cases are allowed to drag on for months and I have dismissed a number where I know the accused person is guilty but nobody has bothered to collect the necessary evidence."

A rooster wandered across to where I sat and pecked in the dust at my feet, pausing every so often to fix me with an inquisitorial eye. Idly I flicked a pebble at him and after berating me with an indignant squawk, he strutted away, presumably to wives and bed. Freddy continued to unburden his soul and it was a sadly familiar story to anyone who knows Africa.

"Corruption," he told me, "has spread from the top and nepotism is rife. The government's socialist policies have driven the country ever further down the economic ladder and although private enterprise is now officially sanctioned, 'management by crisis' is the norm in business. The country is grinding to a standstill. My wife and I are both senior magistrates and we have worked hard to get where we are. The frustrations of trying to prevent ourselves sinking beneath a sea of political chicanery make us both feel that perhaps it is time we turned to some other field of endeavour."

"Politics perhaps?" I ventured quietly. "You might be able to make a difference."

Freddy smiled as he shook his head.

"Oh no, that would be even worse, particularly as neither of us have relatives in high places. No, I will go back to university and take a course in business management so that at least my talents will stand me in good stead, even if it has to be in another country."

We sat on that bench for a long time Freddy and I. Darkness enveloped us and mosquitoes came and went, discouraged by the smoke from my pipe. As he spoke, my heart went out to him, for his is the dilemma faced by any honest man in Africa. I had experienced it in my own country, so had some idea of what he was going through. He wanted to get ahead in his chosen career but to do so meant abandoning his principles and descending to the level of corruption employed by his peers. Yet it is on the shoulders of men and women like Freddy K. Matunga – be they politicians, businessmen or public servants – that the future of the entire continent depends. Competent, educated people are needed, men and women with the conscience, dignity and foresight to recognise what is required by those who depend upon them. There are many such men and women and Africa needs them desperately. Unfortunately they are usually feared by those less able, with the result that, like my friend Freddy, they are wilfully obstructed by the system and eventually leave in search of greener pastures where their talents will be recognised and appreciated.

By the time we went in for dinner, Freddy K. Matunga and I were firm friends. He invited me to hit the fleshpots of Babati with him after the meal but I declined somewhat regretfully. It would have been an opportunity to join in with the locals at play but I was very tired and wanted an early start the following morning.

When I rose at five to resume my journey, I was surprised and not a little touched to see Freddy K. Matunga – resplendent in striped pyjamas – emerge yawning from his room.

"I wanted to see you off," he told me. "You have a long journey ahead of you and it must be a lonely road."

Very much a gentleman of Africa was Freddy K. Matunga and I hope he succeeded in whatever he decided to do. If I read him correctly, whatever it was would have been for his country and the benefit of his fellow Tanzanians.

<hr>

It was a bitterly cold morning when I left Babati, but a few kilometres along the road, I met an itinerant tea seller. A cheerful young man, he carried a large metal pot of the brew, together with three tin mugs and a packet of hard round biscuits. After two cups of sweet, herbal tea and a couple of biscuits, I felt considerably better and while I enjoyed my impromptu breakfast, the tea seller plied me with questions.

When I told him that I wrote for a living, he cheerfully informed me that the Swahili for 'writer' is '*mwandisi ya vitabu.*' I resolved to remember it for future use. I would much rather be referred to as a mwandisi ya whatever than a mere scribe or scribbler. Even the word 'writer' seems pretty mundane beside such a dignified description. English is a lovely language but there are times when it seems to lack a bit of colour.

An interesting distraction to my journey was provided by the playthings, used by local children. These toys ranged from the usual wire and shoe-polish-tin motor cars, tractors and lorries through to beautifully carved wooden scooters and bicycles. Some of these little vehicles were quite rideable and when I was cross with her, I was sometimes tempted to trade Harriet in for a wooden machine. They probably would have been worth a small fortune in Britain and it was only the prospect of riding with wooden wheels on some of the horror tracks I had already encountered that deterred me from such drastic action. Besides, after all we had already been through together, I was falling hopelessly in love with my cantankerous old bike. Apart from teasing me with wheel alignment when I was showing off to Olekwa Ncharo, she had behaved like a real lady and I appreciated her for that.

A somewhat more disturbing aspect of Tanzanian life was the amount of weaponry on view. Even lowly bank messengers carried kalashnikovs and I couldn't help wondering whether they knew how to use them. Wherever I went, there were men walking down the street with rifles slung across their shoulders and none of them wore uniforms to tell me who or what they were. I kept a smile on my face and acted very politely towards anyone carrying a weapon and decided that having been a devout coward all my life, this was not the time to change.

In general, the road between Babati and Dodoma was a bit of a nightmare. The countryside was bleakly uninteresting, the road itself was dusty and badly corrugated, my muscles ached abominably and I was plagued by maddening swarms of flies. I saw few people along the section of the trip and those that I did pass were generally uncommunicative.

The crew of an ancient lorry, broken down on a lonely stretch of road proved to be an exception to this general state of disinterest in my travels. I had been struggling through deep yellow dust and when they hailed me I wondered what on earth I could do to help. At that stage I didn't even know where I was. In the event, they were more worried about my well-being than their own and immediately set about making tea on a small open fire, placed directly beneath the rear of their vehicle. I just hoped there was nothing inflammable inside.

While enjoying the tea – always without milk and very sweet in Tanzania – they questioned me about my journey and rolled their eyes toward Heaven when I mentioned the episode with Christina at Minjingu. I wasn't entirely sure whether their consternation came from my narrow escape from whatever might have happened or my foolishness in turning down such a heaven-sent opportunity.

But both the driver and his mate – I never did get their names – were friendly and cheered me up at a time when I desperately needed cheering. At my query as to whether help had been summoned for their own problems, they laughed aloud.

"Oh no Sir," chortled the driver. "They will know there is something wrong when we do not arrive in Nairobi."

And how long would it take for assistance to arrive? This time it was the driver's mate.

"Maybe two weeks – maybe three; perhaps even one month."

Neither of them seemed to mind, even though such a length of time spent in helpless isolation beside one of the loneliest roads in Africa would have driven the average Westerner to raving insanity. I left them sitting in the shade of their cab and turned to catch their final wave of farewell a good kilometre or so down the road.

I wonder if they were ever rescued.

I had been warned that Dodoma was eight hundred metres higher than Babati, so had been prepared for a climb. What I had not expected was that the countryside was made up of a series of ridges, each one as high or a little higher than its predecessor. Every time I climbed, seemingly into the heavens there was a corresponding descent and then I would climb again. Great exercise perhaps, but hardly what I needed and progress was slow. With lungs bursting and legs feeling distinctly rubbery, I walked up the slopes and after my first few gasping ascents, discovered that enjoyment of my surroundings began to outweigh my fatigue. This was another world, a different face of Africa from the one I knew so well. Here were no vast horizons and no relentless, battering sun. Instead I found cool misty slopes, elegant glades and giant, brooding trees. Creepers, some of them thicker than my arms festooned the branches and both birds and wild flowers were everywhere. On these high ridges I felt a deep sense of peace and time seemed of little import. There were no people and apart from birds and butterflies, my only company was the occasional vervet monkey scampering along the road or peering from the leafy sanctuary of a high branch.

I only spent one night in the mountains and it was not a success. Mist descended early in the evening and I slept with all my clothes on and my teeth chattering against the bitter cold. The one saving grace to that stopover was the uncanny silence that enveloped the countryside as soon as darkness descended. African nights tend to be noisy affairs with night birds, insects and animals blending their voices in harmonious background to the world of darkness. Up in the misty peaks, there was only a primeval silence, so deep that it was almost tangible.

One other night that will live on in my memory for all the wrong reasons was one I spent toiling waterless through a wide, arid plain, north of Iringa. I had almost exhausted my water supplies during the day and so took advantage of the cooler night hours, when I could escape the relentless battering of the sun and my need for liquid sustenance would be less. It was exhausting and very frightening. There was no roadside habitation where I might have slaked my thirst and I was scared to venture off the road in case I managed to get lost. To make matters worse, I was very tired after a long, terribly hot day. Visions of an uncomfortable demise filled my slightly rambling mind and I wondered how long I would last without water. I walked through much of the night, as the road was rough and deeply pitted, conditions that made cycling in the dark almost suicidal. Besides, I no longer had the strength to pedal and while walking, I could at least lean on Harriet.

In the early hours of the morning, I spotted a sheen of water away to my right and stared at it for some time before deciding that it had to be a mirage. Had I been a little more lucid, I would doubtless have realised that such hallucinations are brought on by refraction of the sun's rays, but my mind was far gone from the effects of thirst and exhaustion. When the mirage failed to disappear even after I had identified it, I called out to God and told Him that He was being unnecessarily cruel. I distinctly heard a mocking laugh but the mirage didn't disappear. The mirth was probably that of the *tokoloshe*, doubtless enjoying my painful confusion. Closing my mind to all blandishments, I plodded resolutely onward.

At three thirty in the morning, the mirage changed sides and appeared on my left, this time considerably closer. I stared at it until my eyes ached and slowly became aware of a frog chorus drowning out the silence of the night. This time it had to be real. Laying Harriet down very carefully in the middle of the road, I walked into the bush, my heart hammering and my eyes fixed on the silvery sheen ahead of me. My legs were rubbery with fatigue, my swollen tongue was stuck to the roof of my mouth and thorns tore at my calves, but I hardly noticed the discomfort. It was one of the most frightening moments of the entire trip. What if the water wasn't there? Could I take the disappointment? I didn't know and a hundred doubts, hopes and possibilities vied for prominence in my mind.

I was walking in it before I realised that the water was exactly what it had appeared to be. I was on the edge of a large dam and my shoes sloshed through shallows while a water bird grumbled throatily at having his slumber disturbed. Squatting on my haunches and hardly daring to believe it was happening, I gathered a handful of the liquid and raised it to my mouth for a cautious sip. It was brackish, but it was cold and tasted wonderful. My cracked and painful lips loosened perceptibly under its balm and I felt immediately refreshed. Until then I had been very careful about what I drank, even purifying tap water with the tablets I had for the purpose. This time I abandoned caution and drank until my stomach hurt. Then I filled all my containers and lay full length on my back in the shallows to get my tormented senses together.

In spite of cold water lapping about my shoulders, I dozed and then woke abruptly to drink again. Only those who have experienced real thirst can appreciate the terror it engenders and the sheer wonder of having abundant water available once more. I felt delightfully bloated and remembered to thank God (and the *tokoloshe*) for bringing me to this oasis. I even apologised for the names I had called them both.

As so often happens, once my immediate problems were sorted out, I began passing through villages and tiny kraals, their doors and windows shuttered against the night. Travellers at the roadside raised their heads to murmur sleepy greetings and not for the first time, I marvelled at their fortitude. Believe it or not, these people were waiting for the bus. Public transport in rural Africa is both infrequent and unpredictable, so prospective passengers come prepared for a long wait. When night falls, they merely wrap themselves in blankets and sleep on the ground. At the sound of an approaching engine, it is comical to see heads pop out of blanketed cocoons and check that the vehicle is going in the right direction. If it is, the sleepers leap from their bedding and stand, waving frantically in the glow of the headlights. If

the vehicle fails to stop, the only reaction is a resigned shrug and then it is back to bed.

It was a phenomenon I was to encounter throughout Africa and it did make night riding a little more interesting.

Unfortunately that particular night ride led to a painful encounter with authority the following morning. When dawn broke I was in reasonable shape and spirit despite the travails of the night, so when I pulled up at the gates of Mtera hydroelectric scheme, I had no premonition of trouble to come.

Leaning Harriet against the military guard post, I entered the little building to present my credentials. Inside were two uniformed soldiers in anything but friendly mood. Bloodshot eyes and the smell of stale beer told their own story and as I was scratchy-eyed and irritable after my night on the road, the subsequent interview did not go terribly well.

My travel documents were examined minutely and I was questioned at length. This interrogation was without finesse and seemed to go on and on and on. Each question was repeated with monotonous regularity while my answers became ever shorter and more to the point. Where had I been; where was I going; why was I doing this; was I a spy? Eventually I lost patience and yelled at them, which was hardly sensible in the circumstances. I received a number of painful body blows from angrily wielded kalashnikovs for my sins. Although only half-heartedly administered, they hurt and it was difficult to keep an expression of aloof disdain on my face. I wanted to roll around on the floor and howl at the pain, but I was not going to give them that satisfaction.

When I was finally allowed to go, I was bruised, battered and swearing vengeance. An empty threat of course and the military grins that accompanied my departure showed that everyone knew it. In Africa, he who holds the rifle calls the tune and it behoves everyone else to remain subservient and polite. A lesson I was never quite able to learn.

A further provocation to my temper occurred later in the day as I toiled painfully into Iringa. The first person I spoke to was a policeman who ignored my question about nearby hotels and brusquely requested that I accompany him to see his officer in charge. This worthy – Acting Inspector Gwava – went through the entire gamut of questioning yet again and appeared decidedly dissatisfied with my answers. I had learned my lesson with the soldiers and kept my responses civil, but was unable to account for my whereabouts through every hour of my journey. I carried no map so unless I was in a town, usually had no idea where I was but the acting inspector was not happy with this. Why didn't I carry a map? Why was I using a bicycle instead of more conventional transport? The questions went on and Mr Gwava was obviously getting ever more annoyed. My ribs ached warningly and I tried to keep a smile on my face but it must have appeared somewhat stretched at times.

The acting inspector's suspicions eventually got the better of him and after a few barked commands to his subordinates, Harriet and I were loaded into the local version of a Black Maria – a blue land rover – and whisked away to Police Headquarters to be interrogated by the OCD himself. The initials stood for Officer Commanding the District and this worthy was as suspicious and unsympathetic as had been Acting Inspector Gwava.

The questioning went on and on with boring repetition and my temper grew ever closer to breaking point. I sometimes felt that they were willing me to explode so that they would have reason to lock me up. I struggled to remain calm. In mid afternoon, a Special Branch officer was brought in on the questioning and he proceeded to flatten me completely. After examining my now well-thumbed documents, he smiled beatifically and assured me that there was absolutely no reason why I should remain in the police station any longer.

"I can't understand why you were ever brought in, Mr Lemon," he said pleasantly. "Your papers are in order and you don't appear to have broken any law."

If I hadn't been so astonished, I probably would have lost my temper. It was over four hours since I had been 'arrested' and I was desperately in need of food, a bath and a good long sleep. I explained this with considerable acerbity and it was Acting Inspector Gwava himself who was given the job of escorting me to a suitable hostelry. He took me to an elegantly faded hotel on the main road and left me with strict instructions to 'look after yourself hey.'

Truly Africa is a bewildering place.

Iringa was undoubtedly the most pleasant centre I stayed at in Tanzania. Missy had gone down with glandular fever there during our sixties trip and I had come to know the town and its surroundings reasonably well. Roaming the streets thirty something years later, I was amazed at how little had changed. The roads were tarred, which they hadn't been on my original visit, but they were still wide and lined with huge, smiling trees. The people were friendly and my usual visit to the *poste restante* counter, elicited a big smile from the post office clerk on duty, even if it did leave me letterless.

I spent a cheerful half hour in the municipal market and haggled with the storekeepers like any suburban housewife. This is very much part of the African scene and although it is completely against my nature, Zoe had warned me that if I didn't bargain for anything I purchased, I would be 'ripped off' unmercifully. It had been difficult at first, but once I got into the swing of things, I found myself enjoying the banter involved. Unlike their western counterparts, shopkeepers were seldom offended when a price was queried. They would smile and exclaim with delight, the subsequent haggling often accompanied by tea or a cool drink, laid on by the management.

It was immediately after Iringa that my cycling venture almost came to a painfully premature end. I left the town after a leisurely breakfast and made good progress on an excellent road, all the more welcome for the contrast with the horrific track I had laboured over on the way down from Dodoma. I sang in raucous accompaniment to the hum of the tyres as I sped towards Mbeya and the Zambian border. My troubles were surely behind me and although my ribs still ached from the beating at Mtera, I felt strong and ready for anything.

This was civilised country too, with schools, churches and well-tended fields on both sides of the road. I climbed steadily throughout the day, but for once, it was a gentle gradient and not too demoralising. Children called cheerily from the roadside and I couldn't help wondering whether it was their curriculum or merely the vagaries of teacher training in Tanzania that accounted for the standard greeting of 'Good morning Teacher.'

I had lunch with an excellent fellow called Charles John, who told me that not only was he the only person in the district who could speak English but that he had entertained another long-distance cyclist a couple of years previously. He added the fact that the other chap had been considerably younger than me, but he said it nicely and I was not offended.

I ate well, looked through the family photograph album and allowed myself to be inspected by representatives from most of the neighbouring families, who kept popping in on one pretext or another. I held a photographic session with the John family and then continued on my way, considerably cheered by my little foray into domesticity.

One thing that the people of Tanzania have in abundance is fruit and I reflected as I cycled on that for once in my life, I was enjoying an extremely healthy diet. Oranges, bananas, paw paws, custard apples and the occasional fat avocado pear or coconut made for pleasant eating and while I might have lost a bit of weight, I was certainly keeping fit.

That afternoon went as well as had the morning and as evening drew in, I felt very satisfied with my lot. 'Good morning Teachers' still echoed from the roadside despite the hour, but I had nearly a hundred kilometres under my belt for the day and was approaching a vast, forested area that looked ideal for camping. A large notice expressly forbade the practice but I convinced myself that it could not possibly apply to itinerant cyclists. Breasting a rise, I spotted a likely looking track away to my left and peered through the gathering gloom for the entrance. We began to descend and Harriet gathered speed.

It was a beautifully clear evening. The air was filled with the fragrance of pine forest and my only worry was finding a suitable camp site. We went faster and faster, my soul singing in time to the thrumming of rubber on tarmac.

The pothole was almost a metre across and nearly half a metre deep. I had my neck craned to the left and we were freewheeling at well over twenty-five kilometres an hour when the front wheel dipped, there was a juddering crash and Harriet stopped. I didn't, and my stomach lurched in shock as the road rushed up to meet me. Instinctively I braced for the fall with my outstretched hands but the impact with rough tarmac was horrendous. For a few long moments, everything seemed terribly clear. I distinctly felt the skin tear across my palms and heard the sharp hiss of air escaping from a tyre while my panniers and kit slid haphazardly across the road.

Scrambling to my feet, I was vaguely aware of blood flowing from a number of wounds, but my attention was focussed on my poor bicycle, sprawled forlornly in the centre of the road. The front tyre was flat, and in a state of shock-induced panic I manhandled Harriet upright, collected what I could of my scattered kit and dragged the whole lot off the road.

Only when I was well into the trees and safe from further disasters with traffic did I pause to take stock of my position. Apart from feeling shaky and sick, I was not in too serious a state. My knees and left elbow were leaking badly while my hands were a mess and stiffening rapidly, but I would certainly survive. I took my first aid kit from a pannier before deciding that the damaged wheel had to be my priority if I was to move on before nightfall. Ignoring the pain of my wounds, I turned my attention back to Harriet. Despite hands that were already stiffening up, I managed to remove the front wheel and replace the damaged tube, splattering everything with fat dollops of blood in the process. Lumbering to my feet, I reached for the pump.

It was dark by then but there was an early moon and it shed more than enough light for me to notice what had hitherto escaped my attention. I need not have bothered changing that tube. We were not going anywhere. With a sense of sick despair, I dropped to my haunches once more and surveyed the wreckage of my dream. The impact with the pothole had buckled Harriet's front wheel in on itself to the extent that it appeared almost square.

I felt numb with shock. Before leaving Britain, I had been discussing the matter of spares with a friend.

"I am taking a spare tyre and two spare tubes," I told him blithely. "Of course, if I buckle a wheel that will be the end of the trip, but I can't see that happening."

Brave words – so desperately foolish now that the unthinkable had happened. I had buckled a wheel and my trip – my funny little adventure – was over almost before it had started. Mountain bikes were a rarity in rural East Africa and there was no hope whatsoever of obtaining a replacement wheel rim so far from civilisation. Nor could I repair the damaged one, even if I had the expertise. It required specialist equipment and that surely wasn't to be found in this remote corner of southern Tanzania.

So my dream was over. Instead of covering seven thousand kilometres, I had managed barely a thousand and they had taken me three weeks which was hardly good going. I hadn't even reached Zambia, let alone the

Cape. It wasn't even a partial success. For the first time in my life, I faced total, ignominious failure and I didn't know how to handle it.

Sadly I packed the tools away and reloaded the bike. There seemed little point in tending to my own wounds so I let them bleed. I didn't care. I just wanted to sit down and cry at the humiliation of it all.

Pushing Harriet drunkenly back on to the road, I turned my face toward the south and began walking. The moon gazed benignly down upon us but I was in no mood to appreciate its ethereal beauty. I just walked slowly on, tears coursing down my face and Harriet bumping awkwardly along beside me.

A heavily laden pickup truck roared past me and bitterly I pictured the occupants, warm, comfortable and speeding towards home and hearth. What did they know of my pain and worry? What did they care?

The truck pulled into the verge three hundred metres ahead and I heard doors slam. Through the darkness, I was aware of shadowy figures walking towards me and nervousness clutched at my stomach. Now I was going to be mugged. I reached for the solid comfort of the hunting knife strapped to my waist and carefully undid the retaining clip. If these guys wanted my money, they were going to have a fight on their hands. I might lose what little I had left, but a good punch up would at least give me a focal point for my frustration.

The figures loomed closer and I could see that there were two of them, one very tall and wearing what appeared to be a conical hat. I braced myself for action.

"Are you alright Sir?" Asked a soft American voice and tears of relief welled up in my eyes.

CHAPTER FIVE

(The Missionaries of Kibidulla)

George Ugulumu is an unlikely hero of a venture such as mine but if it had not been for George, my trip would have come to an ignominious end in the highlands of Tanzania.

Dan Butler and Godfrey Chabala had been bringing their families back from a weekend in Dar es Salaam when they were somewhat surprised to see a lone white man trudging forlornly through the night with an obviously damaged bicycle. It was Dan who uttered the softly spoken enquiry as to my welfare and when I mentioned that I had been in an accident, they examined the damage by torchlight. My own wounds were glossed over as 'mere grazes,' but Dan whistled when he ran his hands over the damaged wheel. His words made light of my fears.

"We'll take you back to the farm," he told me. "We have a chap there who might be able to straighten this out. If he can't, you can have the wheel from my bike."

I tried not to show my exasperation, but it seemed important to point out that Harriet was an ATB so a normal cycle wheel would not fit. Dan was unphased and merely gestured to Godfrey to help him haul the bike up on to the overloaded truck.

"Oh we have mountain bikes here too," he murmured with a smile in his voice. "They may not be as good as yours but if you need...."

I was to discover that this was typical of the man. Both he and his son had ATBs far more exotic than my own, but he was perfectly willing to sacrifice his front wheel to a stranger, even though there could be little chance of replacement in Tanzania.

There being no rope available to hold Harriet in place, Dan ensconced himself precariously on top of the load and indicated that I should ride in the cab with Godfrey and the ladies. I was shivering with cold and shock, but it didn't seem right that he should be perched uncomfortably up there while I dripped blood over his nice clean upholstery.

So it was that I arrived at Kibidulla – cold, sore and feeling very sorry for myself, but with a feeling of hope that perhaps all was not yet lost.

Kibidulla was a sprawling mission farm, two thousand metres up in the Tanzanian Highlands. A thriving establishment in colonial days, it had been allowed to lie fallow for years before being taken over by the church of the Seventh Day Adventists. Blessed with a plethora of natural springs, it was being run as a thriving commercial venture and the guiding light behind it was Dan Butler. We were greeted on our arrival by the night watchman, introduced to me as the answer to all my problems.

"George is a bicycle *fundi* – an absolute expert," Dan told me but George's initial reaction to Harriet's woes was hardly encouraging.

"I will try," he promised after examining the buckled rim by torchlight. "But it looks very bad."

I could have told him that and I certainly didn't sleep well that night.

But try George did and with marvellous results. The following morning, he set to work with a spoke key and a rounded stone, wrapped in cloth. Hardly reassuring tools from my point of view but George was my only hope, so I swallowed my misgivings and sat, watching him work in wan sunshine.

I need not have worried. However basic his tools, George Ugulumu was an artist at his adopted trade. The procedure he used was simple, if a little time consuming. First he removed the spokes with the spoke key and then he worked on the rim. Tapping here with the rock, bending there with his hands, sometimes pushing hard against a convenient corner of wall. The alloy was malleable and once the rim appeared vaguely symmetrical, George replaced the spokes and spun it on its brackets. It rocked and wobbled to an alarming extent but he appeared unworried. Out came the spoke key again and he tightened one spoke, loosened another, then repeated the process somewhere else. I lost count of the number of times that wheel was removed, stripped and replaced, but it was well into the afternoon before it began to revolve with any semblance of normality.

Still George was not satisfied. Again and again that wheel came off and the exercise with spokes, key and rock was repeated. At one stage, Dan arrived to lend a hand and the pair of them scrutinised the damaged rim like philatelists poring over a penny black. Dan used his knee to straighten out a particularly vicious kink, then settled down to instruction from George on the art of tightening spokes. Listening to the lecture, I was heartily thankful that I hadn't attempted any repairs on my own account. I might have been able to remove the spokes; I might even have managed to replace them although that is a little more unlikely, but the order of tightening would have baffled me completely. There is a definite sequence to be followed, but even after having it carefully explained to me, I would not have a clue where to begin.

It was late evening when George looked up at me with an uncertain smile. He had toiled throughout the day and by my reckoning had put in at least ten hours work on the bike. This after a night's work with another night to come. That was surely dedication to the task on hand.

"I don't think I can get it any better than that," he told me, spinning the wheel so that I could see there was still a minor vibration. "It should not affect you, provided you do not go too fast."

My laugh sounded somewhat hollow. At the best of times, I could be overtaken by any reasonably energetic tortoise and after this little episode, I certainly would not be travelling at any speed faster than a slow crawl. There were too many potholes about.

Once I was back on the road, I forgot all that but it didn't matter. My front wheel was to shudder and wobble its way along for a further three and a half thousand kilometres. Spokes worked loose in Botswana and there were times when I viewed its erratic perambulations with considerable anxiety, but it would almost certainly have seen the trip through, albeit with a lot more worrying on my part. When I reached Durban however, my mechanically-minded brother in law whisked the wheel away for balancing as soon as he spotted the irregular manner in which it revolved.

Not being sure of the etiquette of the matter, I asked Dan how much I should pay George for his services.

"Ask him what he wants," was his advice. "He loves working on bikes and yours was a brand new challenge so it won't be much."

That was an understatement if ever there was one. The answer to my query took a long time coming from George and I mentally reviewed my finances. I had a couple of thousand shillings on me but could always ask Dan to take me back to Iringa where I could cash a travellers' cheque and...

"Two hundred shillings," George interrupted my anxious thought processes and for a moment, I felt I must have misheard him. The official exchange rate for the Tanzanian shilling was three hundred to the pound sterling and I had obtained mine at twice that.

In effect, George was asking me for thirty pence to pay him for ten hours work. It didn't seem right but Dan's advice was practical.

"He gets half that for a whole day as a watchman and is well paid by local standards. He is happy and it keeps your funds intact so don't worry about it."

I added a plastic watch to George's payment and he seemed very pleased with the tawdry little gift. Harriet's front wheel still has a very faint tremor and whenever I look at it, I am reminded of what must surely be the most excellent and economic example of high-class workmanship I am ever likely to encounter.

Mind you, money means very little in rural Africa. Even Charles John with his large family and relatively affluent lifestyle earned only three thousand shillings (£10) a month as a farm labourer and many of the folk who opened their doors to me along the road earned considerably less than that. As a struggling scribbler, I am frequently on the point of penury but beside these hard working people, I was as rich as Croesus.

Yet food and other commodities were almost as expensive in African shops, as they were in Europe or Amercia. Charles had told me how he intended installing a new floor in his house, yet a bag of cement in Tanzania was retailing at six thousand shillings – two months wages for him. Everyone seemed to get by however, and although their lifestyles were simple and they had little money to spare, most folk were cheerful and happy enough with their lot.

With Harriet back in action and my wounds healing nicely, I was mobile again and prepared for an early start the following morning. Dan's eyes widened when I walked into the kitchen, dressed in my travelling garb of denim shorts and green bush shirt. When I explained that I was moving on, he was horrified.

"Your hands are a mess Man. They need time to form a scab across the wounds or you are asking for infection.

'Besides, your system has taken a hard knock and you need a few days rest."

I did not take a whole heap of persuading. My stomach was playing up and Kibidulla seemed a wonderful place to rest for a day or two. The Butlers were lovely people and I enjoyed being part of a family again, so I was quite happy to extend my stay.

After cleaning Harriet and sorting out my kit, I had time on my hands, so spent it wandering the farm with Dan and assisting where I could. As we worked, he told me of his life in distant Oregon, his faith and his plans for Kibidulla. A fascinating character was Dan Butler.

Probably in his mid thirties (his beard made it difficult to be sure) he had turned his hand to a number of varied enterprises, including fruit picking, tree felling and the running of a vegetarian restaurant. A lean, rangy man, he spoke with the deliberation of a countryman and although his smile was rare, he possessed a sardonic sense of humour, often only apparent by the twinkle in his eye. Dan had picked up the African 'bug' after a stint at Riverside Mission in Zambia and like so many others, he found himself totally smitten by the continent. After Riverside, he and Ellen returned to the United States but couldn't settle, in spite of being home again.

"Everything there is geared toward making more and more money," He told me. "Americans have forgotten how to live."

With two young children in tow, the Butlers returned to the wilds of Tanzania and Kibidulla.

"For all its problems, this country offers far more for youngsters than modern America," he told me seriously. "Here, they have clean fresh air, plenty of space and are not influenced by the horrors of television or video games."

I couldn't help but agree. Missy and I had felt the same when our kids were young and had never regretted bringing them up in Zimbabwe.

"We are happy here," Dan went on. "We don't have much but The Lord provides and the farm is taking shape. There is a great future here for anyone who is prepared to knuckle down and work."

In that, he set a tremendous example to his workers. He worked long hours and was constantly on the move. He had been quick to spot the potential of the springs on Kibidulla and using shovels and muscle power, had installed a network of canals carrying water throughout the two thousand hectares of the farm. These provided irrigation for the maize lands, orchards and a sizeable garden, where Godfrey Chabala ran a school on vegetable husbandry. Dan's visions for the future were without parameter.

"I intend to diversify," he told me one afternoon. "I want to install a cane crushing plant, powered by water or solar energy. I have started a fruit-growing scheme in Mushandike not far from here, where we will operate a training college for the local people. We must teach them to cope with their own crops."

He also had fish farming and cashew nut production on his personal agenda.

"As you know, I've just returned from Dar es Salaam," he said a little sadly. "It was tragic to see thousands of acres of cashews rotting just because nobody had the expertise or the inclination to harvest them. This is an incredibly fertile country, yet people starve because nobody knows how to look after basic crops."

Deeply religious and with the spiritual well-being of the local people as dear to his heart as their physical welfare, Dan had opened two churches, a school and a well equipped clinic on Kibidulla. During my stay, I joined in with family worship and attended a Sabbath day service in the open air, which left me feeling surprisingly uplifted and at peace with myself, even though I have never had much sympathy with organised religion.

Mind you, Kibidulla was a place where anyone could find peace. The Butler's homestead was perched on a rise and looked out over gently rolling hills and ruggedly colourful *msasa* forest that stretched into a hazy blue infinity. It was timeless Africa and good for the most tormented of souls. The garden was planted with tall shady trees and there was a spring in one corner where a gurgling hydram pump diverted crystal clear water to the house itself. Not being of particularly mechanical bent, I had never encountered hydrams before, but they are pumps that are operated by water pressure, so while the springs continue to run, the Kibidulla homestead will always have plenty of water.

The Butlers and other families on Kibidulla lived a real pioneer existence. They had no electricity and everything Ellen used in her household duties, she grew or made herself. Food consisted of fruit and vegetables and as Seventh Day Adventists, the family did not drink tea or coffee – a form of abstinence that was very difficult for me. I have never been keen on any sort of vegetables so mealtimes were vaguely traumatic. I would fill myself with fruit and *ugali* porridge at breakfast and then pick at the spinach, broccoli and other 'delectables' that were put in front of me later in the day. At times I longed for a cup of tea and when I was left on my own one morning, I made a dive for my kit and savoured two delicious cups of the brew. After that little treat, I wandered down to the end of the garden for an illicit puff on my pipe. I felt a little as I had when 'bunking out of school' when I was a boy.

During my stay – and I don't think I can blame the vegetarian diet – my stomach problem worsened dramatically. Ellen dosed me with charcoal but it had little effect and eventually I presented myself before Dr Joshua at the clinic. This kindly Zambian diagnosed amoebic dysentery and prescribed anti biotics, which sorted me out almost immediately. I couldn't resist teasing Ellen about the efficacy of modern medicines as opposed to the homeopathic remedies, she favoured.

"They all have their place," she admitted sweetly, "but it is usually the tried and tested cures that do the trick. Look at your hands."

I couldn't argue on that score. She had applied mellaleuca oil to my injuries and they were healing with astonishing speed. Known as tea tree oil in the west, this is extracted from a tree akin to the eucalyptus, and within two days of the initial application, the hamburger effect on my palms had disappeared and the developing scabs looked pink and healthy.

Although they were the management unit on Kibidulla, Dan and Ellen Butler shared a deep concern for those they lived among and their lives were spent in perfect harmony with the local people. They were Father and Mother to their flock and there was a constant flow of chattering humanity through the homestead. It was wonderful to see blonde and black mixing so harmoniously and I couldn't help feeling that it is with folk like the missionaries of Kibidulla rather than the politicians, do gooders and aid agencies, that the future of Africa lies.

I was sad when the time came to leave Kibidulla and the Butlers. It had been a magical interlude and I envied them their simple lifestyle amid the Tanzanian hills. I envied them their manifest love for each other too. I was captivated by their obvious happiness and couldn't help reflecting that it is a rare quality in our ever more material day and age. It could only have come from their God and the quiet simplicity of the life they led.

"There will always be a place here for you should you decide to return," Dan told me as I made my farewells. "We can build you a cabin among the trees where you can write to your heart's content."

What a tempting prospect that was. How I would love to return to those enchanted hills and loving people. I could find real peace there and perhaps churn out the literary masterpiece that all we scribblers dream of.

On the other hand, I am not sure I could take the diet.

The folk at Kibidulla were not the only religious types I met in the course of my journey. Africa has always been a fertile hunting ground for missionaries and their legacy lingers on in the most unlikely places. Most of those folk with deeply religious convictions that I met seemed to share a contentment with their lot that humbled me and made me wonder a great deal about myself in the reflective moments that occur while cycling.

When I had exclaimed over my luck in being picked up so soon after my accident, Ellen Butler had chided me gently.

"That wasn't luck; it was the work of The Lord," she told me sweetly. "He obviously has plans for you and is guiding the path of your journey."

While flattered to be considered one of the chosen ones, this certainly gave me a different perspective on events and from then on, I made sure I included the *Nkosi Pezulu* in the long conversations and daily planning conferences, held between Harriet and myself.

But the Godly folk of Africa were not all as nice or as pretty as Ellen Butler. I was changing a tube near Serenji in Northern Zambia one evening when I was offered assistance by a young man named Lazarus. He turned out to be a Jehovah's Witness and duly subjected me to the harangue so beloved by those of his persuasion. I am sure their views are very logical and perhaps they are correct in their theories, but they do so much damage to their own cause in the way they go about spreading their particular word. I was grateful for Lazarus' help but in the end I was glad to get away from him and felt both flustered and upset – emotions not at all likely to make me receptive to his views.

Another encounter with Jehovah's Witnesses occurred one hot Saturday afternoon near Ladysmith in Natal and this one was quite comical.

Gonna Subramoney and his friend Robert hailed me from the side of the road as I cycled slowly past. They waved plastic cups at me and with visions of tea or a cool drink, I pulled in for a chat. Both young men had their shirts off and were obviously enjoying themselves. They appeared a little drunk and I was not overly surprised to discover that the cups were filled with whisky and coke, rather than the more usual libations for that time of day. Having said that, I had no hesitation in accepting a generous tot of the Scottish elixir, although I topped mine up with water rather than anything sweet.

Rather to my amazement, these two reprobates also turned out to be deeply religious – or so they claimed - and there followed a hilarious half-hour while they tried to convince me of the error of my ways, while I countered by pointing out that roadside whisky drinking on a Saturday afternoon was hardly behaviour, countenanced by the Good Book, no matter what faith one happened to espouse. We parted as friends and I rode on with Gonna's card tucked into my pocket and a gentle glow of alcoholic beatitude guiding me through the hills of Natal.

One of the sadder aspects of my trip was the absence of wild life in the countries through which I cycled. I did see Oryx, strange looking gerenuk, zebra and a few Thompson's gazelle on either side of the Kenyan border with Tanzania, but the vast herds that used to roam those dusty plains are very much a thing of the past. Zimbabwe was taking its conservation seriously at the time though and I was fortunate enough to see elephant, lion and other animals in the Zambezi valley and Matabeleland. Zambia with its vast areas of undeveloped bush and lack of human population should have been a wild life paradise, but there was little to be seen and the remote hinterland of Tanzania was disappointing in the extreme. In such a sparsely populated portion of Africa, there should have been a wide variety of wild animals on view, but poachers had wreaked their deadly harvest and there was virtually nothing left outside the major national parks. Conservation bodies in the western world raise a great deal of money for the supposed welfare of wild life, but I often feel that they concentrate on the more glamorous animals like lions and elephants, while the smaller beasts are being steadily wiped out by hungry tribesmen.

Yet when I dropped down the Rift Valley escarpment shortly after leaving Kibidulla, I had the feeling of being back in old time Africa – Africa in the raw: that same rugged continent that the pioneers and early white hunters had been so much a part of - the Africa of my dreams. Here it was laid out before me like some huge, pastel painting. Red dust, in places so thick that every movement sent pink clouds drifting through the atmosphere, flat-topped acacias, thorn scrub and the occasional lonely baobab brought a lump to my throat. Hornbills chattered raucously at my approach, a grey lourie cackled his 'go waai' and overall, the heavy, oppressive heat beat down upon the countryside. The sky was a pale, burnished grey and I saw the spoor of various buck and some sort of small cat during the afternoon.

When I stopped for the night, I chose a clearing beside a shallow riverbed for my campsite and as I slipped into my sleeping bag, I had a sense of suppressed excitement in my chest. The fiery red ball of the setting sun dipped behind the trees and I knew in my heart that something was going to happen. I was not to be disappointed.

My camp was close to a large fig tree that was obviously an overnight stop for a troop of baboons. I smiled to myself as I listened to them squabbling gently among themselves. There is something endearingly human about baboons and their family structure is much the same as our own. Jackals yammered their hysterical chorus to the night sky and not too far away, a nightjar trilled it's warbling chorus to the stars.

North of Dodoma, I had been disturbed one night by a leopard wandering around my camp and I wondered whether there were any more in this part of the country. On that occasion, the cat had been noisily vocal which – at the risk of sounding blasé – is always reassuring. The leopard is a silent killer so when he is sounding off, you can be sure he is not on the hunt and sleep soundly in your bed.

With drowsy thoughts of leopards, baboons and travelling nightjars running through my mind, I drifted off to sleep, but the problem when it came was caused by hyenas, which I had heard only infrequently over the preceding weeks.

Two of the brutes wandered into my camp in the early hours and they had obvious designs on my bicycle.

Harriet was propped against a tree some ten metres from where I lay and I awoke to see the slope-backed scavengers advancing on her. Whether their interest was alimentary or sexual, I wasn't sure but the thought of those powerful jaws clamping around the delicate alloy of a wheel rim was more than I could bear. I was out of my sleeping bag like the proverbial scalded cat.

"*Voetsak* – go away," I yelled at the beasts, frantically searching for a stone to throw.

More surprised than alarmed, the hyenas made off and I could hear them snarling, grunting and whining among the shadowy trees. They were back within ten minutes but by then I had armed myself with sticks, stones and anything else that was throwable. For the next hour and a half, I fought a running battle for Harriet's virtue, but those hyenas would not be scared away. Growling and slavering, they kept returning to the fray, their ugly heads held low and swinging from side to side like cagey fighters. I grew hoarse from shouting at them and although my only fear was for my bike, I reflected afterwards that I might well have been at considerable risk myself, had they switched their attentions from Harriet to me.

I ended the night, sitting with my back against my unperturbed bicycle. I still had a few missiles to hand, but my tormenters had finally gone in search of more amenable prey. For the rest of my journey, the merest whimper of a hyena in the night was sufficient to have me out of bed and ready to do battle for the safety and virtue of my travelling companion.

Undoubtedly the unhappiest night of my journey through Tanzania was the very last one. After a long day, I made camp in a small building site some twenty kilometres from the border post at Tunduma. As I retired for the night I was well pleased with myself. I had made good progress throughout the day and was well within reach of my next major objective – the Zambian border, a mere twenty five kilometres further on. Falling asleep, I reflected a little sadly on a tragedy of international politics I had encountered during the day.

A little surprised to see white men working on a brand new highway in black Africa, I had stopped for a chat. They were Yugoslavs and invited me back to their camp for a welcome cup of tea. They were friendly fellows and I enjoyed the hour I spent with them, although I had been fortunate indeed to get the invitation. Lemon's Luck had obviously been working overtime, as the chap I had spoken to initially was the only one in the forty-five strong party who spoke any English at all. He looked ineffably sad as he gave me a tiny peep at the problems that can confront an exile working far from home.

"Some of us are Croats, some Serbs," my friend (for some reason I never did record his name but it was something unpronounceable) told me. "We are out here on two year contracts and before the troubles at home started, we were all good friends. Now our people are fighting each other and there is much tension in the camp. We don't know whether we should still be friends or whether we too should be fighting."

Shaking his head in angry confusion, he went on.

"It is so desperately tragic, my cycling friend. I don't know what can be done as it is all up to the politicians at home."

Tragic indeed and a sad reflection on the times we live in. I left that camp on my last lap to the border, wondering at the unending stupidity of Mankind.

While I was thinking back on my meeting with the unhappy roadmen, I heard a vehicle bouncing through the darkness towards my camp. It moved right into the building site and stopped with the headlights illuminating my resting place. Instinctively I knew what was about to happen.

A voice amplified by a loud hailer broke the silence of the night and loudly informed me that it belonged to the 'officer commanding the whole district' and bade me 'come out with your hands above your head.'

Come out of what, I wondered sourly and cursing the influence of American cinema, climbed a little wearily from my bed. It seemed that Tanzania was not going to let me go too easily.

Indeed it wasn't. The Officer Commanding the whole District turned out to be an overweight gentleman called Gatura. He wore the regalia of a chief inspector and almost immediately accused me of being a spy. My protestations of innocence proved of no avail and once again, Harriet and I were loaded into the rear of a 'Blue Maria' and driven to the police station at Mbozi for questioning.

I later learned that locals had spotted me making camp and reported my somewhat dishevelled appearance to the local constabulary. They could not believe that any white man would forsake the comforts of a civilised home to sleep in the bush so I had to be a 'saboteur-scout.' There was a great deal of excitement among those who had assembled to see me brought in and my kit was spread out on the floor of the little charge office, where it was searched minutely. Questions were hurled at me from all sides, the questioning familiar but following no particular pattern and accompanied by a great deal of heavy handedness. I was punched and pushed from man to man and ended up angry and bruised. The chief inspector (if that is what he was) left the rough stuff to his subordinates while he tried the psychological approach, but his technique was rusty in the extreme. All he did was add to my gathering fury but in a backwater like Mbozi, I don't suppose he had much opportunity to interrogate anyone, let alone a white 'saboteur-scout.'

I grew more tired and more irritable as the night wore on. The police made no attempt to lock me up and the entire interrogation took place in the charge office, the proceedings illuminated by a flickering paraffin lamp and a couple of candles. One raw-looking constable spent ten minutes reading my note books in the gloomy light, but as I have difficulty reading my own writing in broad daylight, I don't suppose he learned a great deal. I bit back a sarcastic comment when he returned the books to me and confined my reaction to a sardonic smile. He didn't even have the grace to look abashed.

There was one moment when panic disrupted the proceedings and might well have led to more serious consequences. It was my own fault too. My kit was being searched for the umpteenth time and as my solid fuel cooker was brought out, I heard someone whisper 'grenade.' It must have been the *tokoloshe* that teased me into precipitately foolish action. Grabbing the tiny stove from the man who held it, I tossed it contemptuously toward the voice and there was a concerted dive for cover, which left me gasping with slightly hysterical laughter.

I received a couple of hefty blows in the kidneys for my foolishness.

It was after two in the morning when my tenuous hold on my own temper finally snapped. I had just been forced to drink all my water 'in case it was poisoned' and quite apart from the attendant discomfort, water was precious to me. I threw a tantrum and ended up with my chest touching that of the OCD and my spittle flecking his face as I shouted at him.

I yelled that I had had enough. He must lock me up, shoot me or let me go. I was a former police officer. I was a British citizen. I knew my rights. I must have sounded as hysterical as I felt and there followed a few moments of stunned silence. Nobody said a word and after absently wiping his chin, the sadly affronted OCD turned on his heel and marched haughtily from the room. He was back a few minutes later and barked out instructions to his gawking rabble.

Still in total silence, my scattered kit was gathered together and packed haphazardly into the panniers. I was then frogmarched from the room.

"Now you have really done it," I told the *tokoloshe* as I was pushed out through the front door of the police station. "You made me ask them to shoot me so they are going to do just that."

Once again I was manhandled into the back of the land rover, to be followed by Harriet, my kit and a young constable called Msiwa who hailed from Kilimanjaro. Chief Inspector (or whatever he was) Gatura glowered from the front seat and my new travelling companion volunteered the information that I was being taken to the border, where I would be handed over to the immigration authorities.

Theoretically I suppose I was being deported without documentation, but the luckless immigration officer who was dragged from his bed to deal with me, didn't have any idea of what to do. Now that I knew I was not going to be shot, I became all rebellious and refused to pay for a bed in a local hostelry. 'You brought me here so you can pay' was my immediate philosophy and eventually the unfortunate immigration officer paid for me to spend the rest of the night in another flea pit, where I managed to snatch a couple of hours sleep.

When the border post opened at seven, I was first in the queue and it was with a feeling of relief that I prepared to leave Tanzania. Looking back on my journey through that vast country, it was a great experience, but I certainly didn't appreciate that at the time. I must admit that in spite of the attendant hassles, I would love to return and explore some more of the place. Although they were desperately poor, the average citizens were hospitable in the extreme, the scenery was spectacular and the weather marvellous throughout. I received a great deal of kindness along the way and encountered much friendly curiosity from those I passed among. I enjoyed time spent at the little wayside tea rooms where men gathered to set the world to rights over sweet herbal tea and *mandazis*, while at wayside *dukas*, I consumed *masodas* – a description covering any fizzy drink – in quantity. My contacts with officialdom often left me angry, frustrated and on occasion bruised, but the notorious border posts were negotiated with a minimum of difficulty. My body had thinned out and hardened over the weeks in Tanzania and after suffering no fewer than nineteen punctures, I was beginning to consider myself an expert in their repair.

Yes, Tanzania had been good to me but on that sunny morning in July, I was only anxious to be out of the place, although I did smile at a set of concrete lavatories outside the border post that had obviously only recently been built. One was labelled 'Men and Women,' while the other was for 'Men Only.' Political correctness and gender equality has yet to arrive in rural Africa I'm afraid.

Yet even the border crossing was not as easy as it might have been. Tunduma is one of those rare spots on the earth's surface where two time zones meet. The result is that although both border posts open their doors at seven in the morning, the Zambian side only start work an hour after their Tanzanian counterparts.

So I spent my last hour in this fascinating country in idle conversation with the Tanzanian officials, all of them anxious for details of my run in with the constabulary. They clicked their tongues in dismay at the rough treatment I had received and roared with laughter when I described my final confrontation with the OCD. The worthy chief inspector was obviously held in particularly low esteem among these fellows and my ever more exaggerated descriptions of his consternation at my outburst, elicited peals of merry laughter.

By the time the gates between the countries swung open, I was almost sorry to be leaving. With a final wave to my new friends who had gathered at doors and windows to see me off, I walked slowly from the Tunduma Customs House and wheeled Harriet into Zambia.

Five weeks on the road and I was into my third country. Despite my weariness, I felt remarkably pleased with myself.

CHAPTER SIX

(Caterpillars and
Hospitality in Zambia)

Cycling from north to south in Zambia is not particularly taxing. It is almost literally all downhill. After
Mpika in the northern province, the Great North Road
follows a steadily descending ridge, which finally drops
away into the escarpment of the Zambezi Valley. There
are occasional climbs, but I found them trivial when
compared with the muscle rending slopes of Tanzania.

The first Zambian I spoke to was an immigration officer who quite blatantly asked what gifts I had for him.
Emboldened by my run in with the constabulary of
Mbozi, I assured him that I carried no *bonselas* for him
or anyone else. He merely grinned at me and didn't try to
make life difficult. It was a harmless little encounter but
it did make me wonder what further official importuning
I was in for. I had heard many stories of official graft and
corruption in Zambia, but have to admit that I experienced no such problems. Roadblock personnel throughout the country were polite, curious and helpful. At one
block, a uniformed constable handed me a folded slip of
paper and the surreptitious way he did it, made me
wonder what was going on. When I examined the paper

later, I found that it contained the fellow's name and address, together with a request that I send him novels, a camera and a signed photograph of Wilbur Smith. I don't suppose Mr Smith does much book signing in Zambia but if he ever reads this narrative, I can point him towards another fan.

The Zambian countryside was totally uninspiring. For eight hundred long kilometres through the Northern Province, the road cut straight, flat and unchanging through what used to be known as MMBA – miles and miles of bloody Africa. The road surface was badly corrugated and as the skin of my hands had split open once more, my juddering progress was extremely painful. I made handlebar 'cushions' with handkerchiefs but the sight of the blood I was losing did nothing for my confidence. There was little habitation and the rivers and streams were all dry, although I was able to keep my water supplies topped up in occasional puddles or at roadside cafes. My main problem was boredom. I found myself missing the rugged grandeur of the Tanzanian hills, completely forgetting the tribulations of life on those lung bursting ascents. In Zambia it was all dry brown scrub and endless forests stretching into limitless horizons.

Nevertheless, the people more than made up for the drab scenery. They were truly fantastic. In that remote area, I don't suppose they saw many strangers apart from those rushing through in modern motor vehicles, so I was something new. Wherever I went, I was surrounded by curious well wishers who fussed over me, plied me with questions and seemed to take strange delight in touching my flesh or my clothing. None of them had ever seen a bike like Harriet and whenever I mentioned that she had eighteen gears, the news was greeted with tongue-click-

ing expressions of astonishment. An n*jinga* with three
'ma-cranks' was luxury indeed, but eighteen – well, that
was just 'too wondrous.' I must admit that I did enjoy
being the centre of attention, while hospitality among
even the poorest of villagers was overwhelming.

Youngsters on bicycles would often ride with me and
appeared to have no difficulty in keeping up, even though
none of their machines boasted even a basic three-speed,
let alone the battery of 'ma-cranks' I was using. Children
still ran out from roadside kraals with shrill cries of
'*mzungu, mzungu,*' their voices as pipingly irritating as
those of their Tanzanian counterparts, but here there were
no begging gestures. The kids merely stood quietly watching me with shy smiles and occasionally giving me a beaming thumb and forefinger salute. I wondered a little about
this gesture and eventually asked a grizzled old woodcut-
ter what it meant. He grinned somewhat slyly.

"The hour has come," he explained, demonstrating
the strange salute for my benefit. I had immediate visions
of long knives and retribution but these Zambians had
gentler motives.

"The hour for a new president," My geriatric inform-
ant cackled. "Kaunda must go."

Soon after my trip ended, Kenneth Kaunda did indeed go. After twenty-seven years of tearful mismanagement, he was ousted in a free and fair election by
Frederick Chiluba of the Movement for Multi Party
Democracy (MMD) whose salutation was the thumb
and forefinger salute.

One hot afternoon in Northern Zambia I came across a
delightful, thatched shelter beside the road, a wooden

bench inside offering unexpected solace for the weary traveller. There being nobody about, I took advantage of the little haven for a rest and a bite to eat.

I was chewing on an old piece of coconut when the local bus drew in and disgorged an elderly gentleman, impeccably attired in grey suit and trilby. We exchanged polite greetings and spoke in desultory fashion before he tipped his hat and bade me farewell. Wandering up an avenue of stunted paw paw trees, he disappeared into a thatched homestead some hundred metres off the road. It was a typical, wattle and daub, Zambian farmhouse and I thought no more about the encounter, pleasant though it had been. Ten minutes later, the elderly gent reappeared. His suit had been discarded and he wore a soft shirt and flannel trousers, together with a tie and comfortable sandals, none of which are normal attire in rural Zambia.

"Would you care for a cup of tea?" He enquired gently and I needed no further invitation. I followed him up to the house and on the way he introduced himself as the Reverend W.L. Membe of the African Methodist Episcopalian Church.

In the yard before the house, a half grown duck was snapping haphazardly around the head of a sleeping mongrel and I paused to watch, fascinated by the strange little drama.

"He is keeping the flies off," the Reverend explained and after studying the scene, I had to admit that he was right. Every time a fly buzzed around the dog's face that little bird whapped it out of the air. I don't think ducks eat flies so what the little chap got out of the exercise, I do not know. Perhaps he just enjoyed being helpful.

The inside of the house was a complete surprise and I paused on the threshold to take it all in. The walls might have been mud, the roof mere thatching grass but in all other respects, that little home was hardly typical of an African country dwelling. A rush ceiling had been installed, there were softly patterned carpets on the floor and the furniture would not have been out of place in any Belgravia penthouse. Heavy chairs with richly brocaded covering, elegant curtaining and a general air of subdued opulence left me speechless. Reverend Membe was obviously pleased with the effect his home had on me.

"All stuff I collected in the course of my travels," he murmured in explanation. It turned out that this re-markable man had spent many years in the diplomatic service of his country, doing stints in Algeria, Germany and the United Nations. On his retirement, he had taken up a piece of land in this remote corner of Zam-bia and settled down to the life of a peasant farmer and itinerant preacher.

"I am happy now," he told me with a smile. "My life is simple. I have a few cows and a well. I work with three different churches and hold my own services for those in the immediate area."

In answer to the obvious question, he shook his head emphatically, a twinkle in his eye.

"Not at all," he said. "I am glad to be free from the stresses of public life. I have a small pension and my needs are few. Why should I miss the rat race?"

For the next couple of hours we chatted over innu-merable cups of tea and I came to the conclusion that the Reverend W.L. Membe is a happy and fortunate man. He has found peace, but only because he had the courage to forsake the trappings of civilisation and return to his roots. How much better the world would be if more people had the sense to follow his example. Instead of which, we allegedly civilised folk push ourselves – and others – to the limit in an increasingly futile quest for money, power and the dubious benefits of a society that seems ever more likely to tear itself apart.

I was particularly intrigued to discover how Mrs Membe had exchanged the fripperies of public life for the basic simplicities of a peasant woman in Africa.

"Ask her," the Reverend smiled so I did. She was shelling groundnuts in the sun and when her husband called her in, she curtsied before me in traditional manner. At my question, her face lit up and she spoke animatedly in the vernacular. The Reverend translated and the smile was still on his face.

"I am free now," she told me. "My only obligations are to my family so I can concentrate on being a wife and a mother rather than a symbol of my country. It is wonderful not to have to worry about appearances."

I can't help feeling that most of us have missed the boat somewhere along the line.

The Reverend was as curious about me as I was about him and time passed pleasantly in animated discussion. More tea and a plate of bread rolls were produced and I gorged myself on the unexpected repast. South African coffee mate was used in lieu of milk and my host smiled when he saw me reading the label. At the time, Zambia was having difficulty in importing anything, let alone such obvious luxuries. Inefficient fiscal policies had left the Zambian kwacha weak and in the shops I visited, there were only a few basic items for sale.

"It used to be a perk of the job," Reverend Membe explained gravely. "Nowadays, imported goods are freely available if one knows where to look, no matter

what our esteemed politicians might tell the peasants."
He would not be drawn on the subject of the approaching election however and I hope and pray that the advent
of a new government in no way disturbed the tranquillity of his life.

Very much a gentleman of Africa was the Reverend
W.L. Membe and when I resumed my journey, I felt
myself rarely privileged to have encountered someone so
obviously at peace with the world around him.

After my unpleasant experience at Mbozi I was wary
about sleeping in the bush for a while and took to going
in to country schools as evening drew in. Although this
invariably made me the focus of chattering attention
from hordes of curious schoolchildren, the teachers
always made me welcome and I slept in classrooms or
offices, usually being invited into someone's home for
the evening meal.

The staple diet of Africa is maize meal – *ugali* or
posho in East Africa and *nshima* in Zambia. In Zimbabwe, we call it *sadza,* but it is all the same thing. During my journey, I ate the stodgy porridge with a variety
of relishes, including an interesting one in Tanzania that
was made from groundnuts and dried pumpkin leaves.
Even to my anti-vegetarian senses, this little culinary
treat tasted delicious. One major problem with enjoying
the hospitality of local people that I encountered was
that wherever I went, I had to eat far more than I actually wanted, as African custom dictates that a host must
finish eating as soon as his guest has sufficed. I don't
have a large appetite, but for the locals, one huge plate
of food was likely to be their entire intake for the day

so I usually forced down more than I needed, wanted or enjoyed.

At Chipungu primary school, I was the guest of Mulwanda Daniel, a young teacher of English and allied subjects. We ate in his dimly lit living room and he glanced at me somewhat hesitantly as he laid out plates for supper.

"Do you eat caterpillars?" He asked and I shrugged a little uncertainly.

"I am willing to try anything," I told him and he smiled in obvious relief.

The grubs were served fried and eaten as an adjunct to the main dish of *nshima* and vegetable relish. They were small, shrivelled and hardly appetising to behold, although they proved surprisingly palatable. I swallowed the first couple without daring to chew, but seeing that my host had no such compunction, I managed to bite down firmly on one whole caterpillar. It was juicy and once I got over the initial repugnance of the western palate, quite tasty. Mulwanda was obviously pleased with my reaction and after the meal, gave me a bag of grubs to take with me. I am ashamed to admit that in the cold light of day, the caterpillars proved more than I could face and I spread the entire repast on the ground for the benefit of passing starlings.

Entering Isoka, a sign at the roadside made me choke with semi hysterical laughter.

'Please avoid AIDS,' Proclaimed the sign in large black letters. 'Welcome to Isoka and Happy Loving.'

In Africa, even the gravest of problems takes its rightful place in the even tenor of daily life.

My days passed pleasantly enough and I dropped steadily down through the country, averaging a little over eighty kilometres a day. One hot afternoon, I stopped to chat with a young charcoal burner in a very isolated kraal. He offered me a share of the lunch he was spooning enthusiastically into his mouth from a metal plate. It looked like a dish of potatoes in insipid gravy and I recoiled a little from the sour smell that emanated from it. I declined the offer and so that he would not feel in any way offended, asked for a drink of water. A bowl of dirty brown liquid was produced and I chided myself for being so considerate. The water smelled worse than had the potatoes but I couldn't very well refuse it. With memories of my amoebic dysentery very much in mind, I sipped tentatively at first, but I was thirsty and eventually drank the lot. The water tasted as bad as it smelled but I suffered no ill effects and could only assume that by that stage, my beleaguered system had become immune to the assorted nasties, I kept inflicting on it.

As my encounters with humanity grew more sporadic and I spent more and more time on my own, I found myself beginning to shun contact with my own kind. Unless I needed water, I sneaked past isolated kraals and only greeted those few folk I encountered after they had hailed me first. I don't know whether this is normal behaviour among those who wander through lonely lands, but it certainly worried me for a time.

On one occasion, I took my anti social attitude to ridiculous extremes. I had a rear wheel puncture at the time and virtually carried Harriet around a kraal where a chap was actually repairing the tube on his own bike.

Rather than take advantage of the occasion, I shunned the possibility of assistance and repaired the damaged tube a little further on in proud and lonely isolation.

Even for me this seemed pretty ridiculous and it made me wonder whether I really was losing my marbles. Could I be going completely mad? Everyone in Zambia had been so nice to me yet I was avoiding them all as though they were lepers. Perhaps it was me who had the leprosy – in the mind at any rate.

As I drew closer to Kabwe and the outskirts of civilisation, I grew increasingly nervous and wondered how I would cope with the normal world.

One evening when I was still about eighty kilometres short of the town I once knew as Broken Hill, I was cycling through well-tended farmland when another cyclist drew up beside me and introduced himself as Eric Kingsley Nyirenda. In the course of conversation, Eric proudly volunteered the information that he was the owner of a nearby tavern. When I questioned him about this establishment, it transpired that due to a temporary cash flow problem, the tavern was not actually open for business but Eric intended to start up as soon as he made a bit of money from his maize crop. As maize production had been poor throughout Zambia for the previous four seasons, Eric was not particularly sanguine about an imminent opening.

"Where are you going to sleep tonight?" He asked the inevitable question but it was still early and I hadn't given the matter any thought. He pointed out that the farms on the left hand side of the road were all owned by white people, who would surely give me a bed for the night, but I wasn't interested. The prospect of clean sheets and civilised food was tempting, but I had no intention of inflicting my company uninvited on anyone – not even my own kind.

A little shyly Eric asked whether I would like to spend the night at his village.

"You can sleep in my tavern if you like," he offered and so it was arranged. We left the main road a little further on and soon arrived at Eric's basic little home.

The tavern was merely a derelict building with graffiti-covered walls and much evidence of rats on the floor. It did not look inviting but I diplomatically agreed that with a great deal of work, it could show potential. I declined to sleep there however and it was decided that I should make my bed on Eric's veranda. His wife was away in Lusaka for the night so the arrangements were quickly sorted out.

On the pretext of showing me around, Eric wheedled a ride on Harriet and we set out on a triumphal tour of the neighbourhood, mounted on each other's steeds. I was surprised at how difficult it was to ride an ordinary upright bicycle after weeks spent on my ATB and could only admire the locals for the manner in which they travel vast distances on these very basic machines.

We called in at a beer drink where I ventured a cautious sip (or two) of the local brew, but it was far too potent for me and I declined to get involved in a boozing session. We left to a chorus of good wishes and ribald advice from the assembled imbibers, some of whom looked as though they had been at the beer drink throughout the day.

It was dark when we returned to Eric's house and I busied myself setting up my bed while he lit the fire for supper. I heard him shout something to one of his sons and a few moments later, the young man staggered off into the night with a large bag of maize on his shoulder.

"Where is he going?" I asked innocently, only to find myself horrified and touched by Eric's reply.

"I know all you *wazungu* like steak," he told me lightly. "There was a cow killed today in a nearby village so I have sent him to barter the grain for some meat."

At my protest, he was adamant.

"You are my guest," he told me sternly. "You like steak so in my house you will eat steak."

It was as simple as that. The meat was brought, cut into strips and roasted in the flames. We ate it charred, tough and stringy, but the generosity of Eric's gesture made it into a finer treat than any filet mignon or beef Wellington, served in classier establishments. In famine-torn Zambia, a bag of maize represented food for a fortnight in the average household, yet Eric had given this away for the benefit of an itinerant stranger. By any standards it was a noble gesture.

After supper, we sat up late around the fire, setting the world to rights beneath the deep purple panoply of the night sky. I lit up my pipe and gave Eric a handful of tobacco, which he mixed with a weed of his own and wrapped in newspaper to make an inelegant cigarette. At my enquiry, he proudly produced a potted *dagga* or cannabis plant and offered me some of the ground up leaf. He told me that all the locals grew their own plants and although such cultivation is against the law, the police turned a blind eye to the practice.

"We feed them when they are on patrol," he explained. "They all smoke the *dagga* themselves so it would not be in their interests to uphold the law is these cases."

It is a practical philosophy that to this day is in use throughout the rural areas of Africa. *Dagga* is freely available and part of life. There is almost no use of hard or addictive drugs and if smoking the weed alleviates the harshness of everyday living, then this state of affairs surely cannot be a bad thing. I didn't take advantage of Eric's offer but I could certainly sympathise with his need for the little comfort.

He really was a gentleman at heart, Eric Kingsley Nyirenda and his generosity with that awful steak left me humbled and very touched.

An unforeseen problem I was struggling with on this section of the trip was the extreme cold whenever the sun wasn't out. I can probably describe it best by quoting from one of my journal entries at the time.

31st.July

'The mornings are desperately cold and of course I didn't think to bring gloves with me. This is the African summer damnit! It is supposed to be hot, yet I start off at first light with my track suit over my clothes and a scarf wrapped around my face. My bush hat perches atop this ensemble and I probably look totally daft, but I am usually too cold to care. Besides, there is nobody about at that hour to see me. As soon as the sun rises, I stop for tea and the biggest difficulty is in getting the stove going. My solid fuel tablets are kept in reserve for an emergency so with fingers numb from the cold, I fill the stove with twigs and then struggle to keep violently trembling hands still while lighting a match. How blissful it seems when the fire is going and I can warm myself to a degree. Even better when the tea is ready. On occasions, my patience runs out and I don't even wait for the water to boil, just drinking it warm with plenty of sugar.'

The days themselves were often blustery and the wind usually blew straight into my face. After two and a half weeks, the novelty of Zambia and its friendly citizens was definitely beginning to pall. The general boredom of the countryside and the unfriendly weather were taking their toll and there were times when I struggled to maintain my enthusiasm for cycling through Africa. After all, what was I trying to prove and to whom? I could take a train to Cape Town and nobody would know the difference.

I would though, and that was not a pleasant thought so I pushed myself ever onward. After my initial roadside cup of tea, the morning sun would feel balmy on my skin and when the wind wasn't blowing. I would whistle or sing my way along in raucous disharmony with the birds and insects, life seeming like a generally pleasant adventure. Then as the day wore on, the heat would build up and sweat would spring from my pores, stinging my eyes and making life generally uncomfortable. The birds and insects would take themselves off for a shady siesta and by early afternoon, I would be cycling through a cauldron of steamy silence, feeling totally disgruntled with my wandering life.

Sometimes I too would siesta beneath a shady tree, but I would invariably find myself under siege from mopani flies and other annoying little insects so I didn't make a habit of it. More often than not, I merely cycled on through the hot part of the day, sweat streaming down my face and my eyes struggling to cope with the harsh glare of Africa. Even though I was now very fit and the gradients were gentle, my muscles seemed to creak with the strain of merely keeping me going and almost tangible visions of ice cream and cold beer danced through my mind in a masochistic form of torment.

My cycle ride to Cape Town was supposed to be fun damnit!

CHAPTER SEVEN

(In Trouble Again)

It was terribly hot, I was tired and I had another puncture. My score was in the high twenties now and I cursed
monotonously as I worked. Sweat ran into my eyes as
I removed the wheel, stripped off the tyre and removed
the inner tube from the rim. My panniers and bedroll
were scattered around me, birds chattered half-heartedly
in the treetops and I was vaguely aware of the shrill
squealing made by numerous cicadas. I was far too hot
and far too fed up with life to appreciate the sound track
of Nature and I concentrated on what I was doing.
I hadn't seen another vehicle in hours and might well
have been alone in the world.

I didn't notice them at first or if I did, merely took
them for the usual gawkers attendant on any stop that
Harriet and I made in Zambia. People loved to gather
around and pass comment on the strange yellow *njinga*
and the equally weird *mzungu* using so unusual a form
of transport.

I was too hot and irritable to pay much attention to
spectators and only reacted when I realised that one of
the bystanders was rummaging through a pannier.

"Hey, what do you think you are doing?" I shouted
angrily, dropping the wheel and marching toward the

rummager. It was then that I realised I was surrounded by seven young men. Two of them carried pangas, another had a small axe slung across his shoulder and the rest were armed with long sticks. As I leaped to my feet, they moved to encircle me and I stopped, suddenly very wary. I had read many reports of robberies in Zambia and this was a lonely stretch of countryside. I wasn't frightened but I was angry with myself for getting into such a situation. Moving slowly, I backed up until I could feel Harriet comfortingly against the back of my legs.

"We want money," the smallest and scruffiest of the bunch informed me. He spoke hesitantly and looked as though he was trying to be tough. Although very short and weedy looking, his diminutive size was more than reinforced by the panga in his hand. I did a quick mental round up of my resources.

Before I left Britain, Lace had sewn pockets into my sleeping bag as well as a pannier and it was in these that my US dollars and sterling were stored. I had travellers' cheques in the moon bag around my waist and about a thousand Zambian kwacha (which didn't amount to much) in my pockets. I could see little chance of escaping from these young thugs so I slowly withdrew my purse, took out a handful of kwacha and tossed them to the little spokesman with as much nonchalance as I could muster. He remained where he was with his eyes on my face while one of his cronies scrabbled in the dust for the discarded notes.

"We want more than that," he suddenly insisted, but seemed totally at a loss when I assured him that I had no more in the way of hard cash.

"I only carry travellers' cheques and for those, you will have to come to the bank with me."

He hesitated and there was muttering among his henchmen.

"What about American dollars?" Another one gritted menacingly. His assumed toughness did not quite ring true and I decided that he was far more nervous than I was. None of them seemed to know what to do next.

"I don't have any dollars," I told them. "Only kwacha and I have given you those."

"Give me your watch," it was the leader again and this put me in a quandary. Although not particularly valuable, the watch had been a parting gift from Lace and held considerable sentimental value. I unbuckled it from my wrist and held it up so that they could all see it winking in the sunlight.

"I would give you this watch with pleasure," I told them in the tones of a Fagin lecturing his band of cut throats, "but there is not another watch like this is in all of Zambia and you would soon be arrested."

This was a blatant lie as it was an inexpensive Sekonda but I could hear a distant rumble and my spirits lightened at the prospect of rescue.

"See," I held the watch up toward the leader. "It has a special message written on the back so that it can quickly be found."

He moved eagerly forward to have a look at this example of modern technology. The others all had their eyes fixed on the magic timepiece and I pushed my way out into the road, almost bowling the leader over in the process. Much to my relief, a container lorry was bearing down on me in a cloud of dust and I waved frantically with both arms.

Brakes squealed and more dust spewed from the wheels as the huge vehicle shook itself to a halt. As it pulled up, my would-be assailants melted into the bush. Gabbling a little from nervous emotion, I explained the situation and both the driver and his mate climbed down from the lorry, leaving it to tick over as they contemplated my dismantled bicycle.

"Don't you want us to take you on to Kabwe, Bwana," the driver offered as I worked. "There are many *tsotsis* along this road and you will be safer with us."

I assured him that I would be fine, they wished me well and repairs completed, I rode on. The lorry moved slowly behind me for a couple of kilometres, then overtook and disappeared into the distance, my grateful wave answered by friendly blaring on the hooter.

I had been very lucky. Thanks to Lace's foresight, I hadn't lost any real money and my kit was intact. I felt a little ashamed at having handed over my kwacha so limply, but consoled myself with the thought that I hadn't really had a choice. If I had tried to resist, I could have taken a bad beating. I reported the incident at Serenji police station, but the constable taking my report was unenthusiastic and I couldn't blame him. I had lost only cash, couldn't describe my assailants and would not be around should arrests be made. I couldn't even pin point the site of the incident with any certainty. He took a brief statement but I don't imagine the enquiry went any further than that. I hadn't even thought to take the names of the lorry crew.

There were two amusing albeit indirect sequels to that little drama. I still had a few kwacha left in my pockets and on my arrival at Mkushi River the following day, totted up my resources to see whether I could afford tea and toast. I had three hundred kwacha which ought to have been ample so thankfully ensconced myself on the hotel veranda, where I did full justice to a plate of the necessary. The bill when it came was for exactly three hundred kwacha and as the usual charge for such a repast was around fifty, I queried it with the waiter. He took me in to see the hotel accountant who regarded me with obvious disfavour.

"What is the time?" he asked – a little irrelevantly it seemed to me.

"One thirty."

"Lunch time?"

"Of course," I muttered irritably, "but what has that...."

"Then that is for lunch."

He pointed to the bill and I turned away, knowing that argument was futile. Had I ordered my sustenance either side of the official lunch hour, I would have been charged for tea and toast, but at lunch time, everything eaten was lunch and there was no disputing the matter. It was a hard lesson in African economics.

Completely penniless and determined to time my tea breaks properly in future, I cycled on toward Kabwe and an opportunity to cash a travellers' cheque. The following day was Saturday and being unsure of official banking hours, I made an early start and cycled hard to be in town before everything closed for the weekend. The road was a good one and I was fairly flying along when a land cruiser stopped and a white man stuck his head out of the cab.

"You look in one hell of a hurry," he commented mildly. "Are you actually enjoying yourself or can I offer you a lift into town?"

I was slightly confused because he was facing in the wrong direction but he said that he had already passed me and then felt guilty about not offering assistance.

I explained my predicament and was soon sitting beside him in the cab while Harriet sprawled stylishly in the back.

Thus I came to meet Don Burton. On learning that I hailed from Zimbabwe, he mentioned that he had a brother farming there. I knew Ken Burton well, so all thoughts of banking in Kabwe were forgotten and I went back to Mufandzalo Ranch for the weekend.

It was over a week since I had bathed and nearly three since I had eaten anything other than indigenous food – and then only vegetables. I was unshaven, dirty, probably somewhat smelly and more than a little hungry. In fact, I wasn't fit to mix with civilised people at all, but Don's wife Maryanne made me welcome as only farming folk can do. After I had showered, shaved and changed into the blessed relief of clean-ish clothing, I wandered into the kitchen where she was hard at work. The smell of baking bread made saliva spring to my mouth and I breathed in appreciatively.

"Have a bread roll," this wonderful woman offered. "I've just taken them out of the oven."

I needed no persuasion. Maryanne sliced two rolls in half, spreading them liberally with farm butter while my mouth literally watered. All thoughts of *nshima*, caterpillars or exotic vegetable relishes were forgotten while I concentrated on those dripping, golden relics of a world I had been out of far too long. I tried hard not to stare while my hostess prepared the feast and then I took the rolls out into the garden with a cup of tea. There followed five minutes of the most exquisite, self-inflicted torment I have ever experienced.

Putting the plate carefully on to a bench, I sat on the lawn in front of it and sipped slowly at my tea, my eyes fixed on the rolls and taking in every delicious, honey-covered curve. The fragrance of fresh bread filled my nostrils and my body trembled with anguished anticipation.

"I am going to eat yooou," I crooned to the hapless rolls, feeling an enormous sense of power and pride in my own self-control. I longed to wolf them down, but then they would be gone and there would be nothing to look forward to. While I gazed at the rolls, they were a treat in store and could be savoured to the full.

And savour them to the full, I surely did. I eventually took a very small nip at the crust of one roll and then of course I was lost. Within moments, the plate was clean and I was left with a delicious aftertaste in my mouth. Regretfully, I took the crockery back to Maryanne in the kitchen and she smiled.

"Like some more?" She offered. "There are plenty there and they all have to be eaten while they are fresh."

"No, that was ample," I assured her but I lied. I could have eaten every single roll she had baked and still had room for more, but I didn't want to appear too much of a glutton. Somewhat hastily, I returned to the safety of the garden before I was tempted to change my mind.

⚜

Once again I was part of a family. The Burtons lived in rather different style to the Butlers of Kibidulla but they also made me feel totally at home and pleased to share something infinitely precious – even if only for a short time. With my own children long out of the nest and Missy and I parted, I missed the curious empathy that exists in families and had not even been aware that I was missing it.

Don Burton raised hardy Boran cattle on his two and a half thousand hectare ranch. He and Maryanne were both Zambians, born and bred with no plans to leave the country.

"It is the only place I can make a decent living doing nothing," he told me with a grin but the amount of work I saw him put in, both on the farm and on behalf of his employees belied the jocularity of his words.

"Things are coming right in this country," he told me in a rare moment of seriousness. "We have gone through our bad times and there were many moments when I felt like quitting, but we are getting support from the government now and at last we can make a decent living. We can get whatever we need and do what we like with our own money, so that Zambia has once again become a wonderful place to live and raise a family."

It was a sentiment echoed by other Zambian farmers I was to meet over the weekend and once again I was a little sad when it was time to move on.

The Burtons were to play a further part in my story but I didn't know that when I thanked them both and kissed Maryanne in farewell. She had given me rolls, fruitcake and boiled eggs to help me on my journey and she chided me gently on my eating habits.

"Mind you eat it all today," she scolded smilingly. I had told her how I liked to eke out my supplies, particularly when I had something nice to look forward to. In fact, that little hamper was to last me the three days it took to cross into Zimbabwe and I enjoyed every mouthful.

One striking anomaly about Zambia was that even after more than three decades of independence, I was still addressed by most people as 'Bwana' or 'Sir.' It seemed terribly colonial but probably had more to do with my advanced age than the colour of my skin. In East Africa, I had just about grown accustomed to being called '*Mzee*' although it had taken me a while to realise that I was the person being so addressed. In Zimbabwe it was to be '*Madhala,*' so the Bwana was almost certainly in the same vein. All the same, it was nice to think that it might have been a relic of the well-mannered society my colonial forbears tried to create in this little corner of Africa. Good manners and respect for one's elders seem to have been largely forgotten in the western world, but they have always been part of the African scene. Old fashioned though it might sound, I hope things stay the way they are.

Yet still there was no wild life to be seen. In that sort of countryside, I might have expected to spot elephant and most of the larger plains game, but it seemed that poaching had denuded the country of what was surely the heritage of every Zambian. I had been assured at Mufandzalo that animals of all sorts were still plentiful in the Luangwa Valley, but that was well off my route and I saw nothing larger than the occasional scampering mongoose. It all seemed very sad, but I put it down to the general tragedy of Africa, although Zambia seemed to have suffered more than most other countries. I couldn't really blame the Zambian tribesmen either, even though they were the instruments of the mass destruction of species. For most peasants, anything on four legs was either food (the word for antelope throughout Africa is '*nyama*' – meat) or a danger to himself or his crops. Thus the average peasant felt entirely justified in killing any beast he encountered. As the human population of the continent increases, so will this situation worsen. Africa has the fastest growing population in the world today and soon all the wild animals will be gone. Sociologists call it progress!

From one point of view, Zambia was an incredibly difficult country to cycle through, even though the terrain was relatively flat and distances between centres of habitation not nearly as vast as they had been in Tanzania. At least there I could plot my progress, while in Zambia there were no hills from which I could view my surroundings and no kilometre pegs or road markings. I sometimes wondered whether I was moving at all. I knew this was only an attitude of mind and repeatedly told myself off in the strongest possible terms for making difficulties where there were no difficulties. It didn't help at all. In fact, the general boredom of my surroundings coupled with the apparent lack of progress was totally exhausting.

In Tanzanian hotels I had been allowed to pay for my accommodation in the local currency, but that was not the case in Zambia. At the Crested Crane motel in Mpika, US dollars were demanded in quantity and that made a substantial hole in my finances. I remembered the motel from the 1963 trip and in those days it had been a comfortable hostelry with excellent food and friendly service. That situation had certainly changed for the worse. The management were abrupt to the point of rudeness, my room, although clean was sparsely furnished and the food was barely edible. The bar didn't open in the evening and the place was without water for much of my stay. A large bathtub resting grandly in the centre of the front lawn seemed eloquent testimony to the run down nature of the place and I was glad to leave after an uncomfortable night. From there on, I took to sleeping in the bush and taking advantage of schools or private accommodation when it was offered along the way.

Lusaka was like any other city in Africa – crowded, dirty and frenetic. Salesmen offering jewellery, curios and exotic adventures clustered around me as I rode into the centre of town. Their importuning was almost frantic but when I shrugged off their blandishments, they seemed in no way put out and merely moved away in search of other victims. I arrived in town fairly early in the morning and had a brief look around the shops, but was unimpressed. I never have been the shopping type and Lusaka certainly had little on display to recommend it. Checking for mail at the central post office, I was approached by a slim, good-looking man with a Canadian accent.

"Are you that guy who is cycling from Nairobi?" He enquired and – a little surprised – I admitted that indeed I was 'that guy.' He introduced himself as Frank Fournier from Riverside Mission and explained that Dan Butler had sent a message down from Kibidulla with a request that he look out for 'a crazy Zimbabwean cycling down the continent.'

I was only too pleased to rescue my bicycle from a youth who had kindly offered to look after her – for a price – and enjoy a lift with Frank to the mission, Harriet reposing comfortably in the rear of his truck.

I spent the night at Riverside Mission with Frank and his teenage son who was visiting from Canada. Once again I struggled with the vegetarian, no-tea-or coffee diet, but it was comfortable and like Kibidulla had a lovely atmosphere about it. Everyone in the mission was friendly and curious as to what I was doing and I made a lot of new friends – who of course I am never likely to see again.

One remark Frank made during the evening will always stick in my mind.

"All the white Zimbabweans I have met," he told his son, "have been exactly the same."

I braced myself for the usual witticism about overweight, beer swilling ex Rhodesians that white men from my country grow accustomed to when travelling abroad, but Frank had no such aspersions in mind.

"They have all been tall," he went on thoughtfully. "They speak softly and are always seeking new horizons and looking for adventure."

It was a lovely comment and I preened inwardly, but a fortnight later, I watched white Zimbabweans being sick in a Kariba gutter. They had drunk too much over a holiday weekend and I was thankful that Frank wasn't there to witness the shattering of his ideals.

Riverside was nice, but I was close to home now and anxious to be moving on. I rode hard the following day and in the late afternoon found myself dropping down the escarpment into my beloved Zambezi Valley. There were no animals to be seen but the searing heat and vast mopani forests made me feel instantly at home. I intended to cross the border at Kariba, feeling that as it was less frequently used than the Chirundu crossing, it would be quieter and – being my hometown – less likely to present problems with officialdom. I was way off beam on that score but had no inkling of troubles to come when I made camp among the trees on my very last night in Zambia.

Harriet posing with the John family.

George and I with the buckled wheel.

A typical Tanzanian tea room.

Inside – Mandazis and man talk.

By the time I reached it, I had forgotten.

Fellow cyclist in Harare.

Depressing repairs in the wet and windy Cape.

Spectacular Cape countryside.

Cherokee Chief in Tsitsikamma Forest.

Made it – looking up at Table Mountain.

CHAPTER EIGHT

(Homecoming of a Wanderer)

I should have known that Zambia would not let me go any easier than had Tanzania. Packing up my camp on my last morning in the country, I was bubbling with excitement at the prospect of reaching Kariba and the home of Brian, my eldest son. It was a moment I had dreamed about since leaving Nairobi – my very first major goal. My thoughts were a kaleidoscope of fantastic imaginings as I placed the loaded panniers on my battered bike. I had phoned Missy from Riverside announcing the date of my arrival and pictured myself arriving in triumph to a rapturous welcome from my assembled family. I could even put up with a little media coverage and wondered whether anyone had thought to inform the newspapers. Perhaps I could persuade someone to photograph Harriet and I crossing the dam wall. That really would be one for the souvenir album and I savoured the thought.

After the initial excitement of my arrival, I looked forward to sitting down with the whole family to a slap up meal of steak, egg, chips and ice cream, all washed down with a cold beer or three. It was a prospect to be savoured but the reality was very different.

It had been a reasonable night although my sleep had been disturbed a little before midnight by a truck moving slowly along the main road. The ambulatory speed of the vehicle and the way a powerful spotlight played among the trees told their own story and my heart seethed with anger as the vehicle disappeared into the night. No wonder there were no animals left. What chance did they have against these butchers of the bush? These were not mere tribesmen looking for meat to feed their families. These were the commercial poaching fraternity with their vehicles, their spotlights and their high-powered rifles. A totally different breed and one with which I could never come to terms. For an hour or so I listened for a shot but heard nothing and when the truck finally returned along the road, I offered a prayer to whatever Deity might have been listening that they would remain empty handed for many nights to come.

Apart from that incident, it felt wonderful to be back on the valley floor and when daylight seeped through the trees, I lingered over tea and the last of Maryanne's fruit-cake. As water boiled on a fragrant mopani fire, the early morning atmosphere of the great forest invigorated me and I looked forward to the day ahead with ever increasing enthusiasm. A flock of red-billed buffalo weavers – *bubalornis niger* to the ornithological types - chattered harshly at my presence and I smiled at the sound. These noisy little creatures are known as '*sheka mfazi*' – chattering women – among the rural people of Zimbabwe, but their harsh and noisy outpourings made me feel very much at home.

Setting out with the early morning sun, I whistled and sang my raucously tuneless way along the valley floor and even dared to wonder whether I could make Kariba by mid morning. I should have known better. Life on the road with David Lemon is never that straightforward.

I had covered less than ten kilometres when I had my first puncture. It was in the rear wheel and was followed by another one less than two kilometres further on. My excitement at imminent homecoming rapidly dissipating, I changed the tubes and as the rear tyre was worn to a delicate thickness, replaced it with the one that had been resting on top of my kit ever since Harriet and I had left Nairobi. The worn one had done me proud and it felt like saying goodbye to a friend when I buried it in thick bush well away from the road. We had been through a great deal together that tyre and me.

I was fifteen kilometres from Siavonga, the town on the Zambian side of the dam wall when the front tyre went down. Three punctures, only two spares and it was already far too hot for rubber work repairs. Having pondered the problem, I tried pumping the tyre to its maximum capacity and pedalling like billy-oh in an effort to get as many kilometres behind me as I could before the tyre went down again. All very well in theory but the intervals between pumping became ever shorter and eventually I gave up and walked, pushing the crippled bicycle along the tarmac. I was climbing by then, so would have been reduced to walking in any case but it was hot and frustrating work. By mid morning – the time I had hoped to reach Kariba – my early sense of euphoria had entirely evaporated.

My last hill in Zambia put all its predecessors to shame and my legs felt as soggy as my front tyre as I climbed. The road went up and up and up, the gradient increasing in severity with every forward metre. Sweat streamed down my face and I found myself heaving for breath but at last I was over the top and there in front of me was Lake Kariba. In a state of considerable excitement, I sat down under a tree and put pen to paper in my journal.

16th August
'Looking out across the incredible deep blue expanse of Kariba, I feel a great big lump in my throat. Of all the places I have seen in this wonderful world, Kariba holds the most marvellous memories for me. It is home. It is a place I love and the place I would like to die in. Suddenly the traumas and difficulties of my morning and the rest of the trip are forgotten. I am almost there and my heart is thudding with excitement.'

Lake Kariba was born on 3rd December 1958 and reached its optimum area of five and a half thousand square kilometres in 1963 – the year Missy and I had passed through with her family. She had immediately fallen in love with the lake and we had both been overjoyed to be transferred to Kariba early in my career with the B.S.A. Police. Over succeeding years, I spent much of my time exploring the lake and its surrounds, while in 1985 I became the first – and still the only – person to row an open dinghy from one end of the lake to the other and back again. Four years later, I had skippered that lovely old Kariba schooner, Queen and we had enjoyed eighteen glorious months of wandering around the islands with excited tourists and generally enjoying ourselves. I suppose it wasn't surprising therefore that I was a little emotional as I gazed across that vast blue expanse and reflected that I was almost home.

But first I needed my tyres repaired. I still had a pocketful of unspent kwacha that would be of no use to me anywhere other than in Zambia, so I decided to call in at the first garage and save myself the hassle of repairing my own punctures. After the rigours of the morning I felt that I deserved the little treat.

I had the job done at a well-stocked establishment on the outskirts of town and then set out to spend my remaining Zambian cash in the grand manner.

I have always felt that I could cope with the problems attendant on having a great deal of money, but rarely have a chance to prove the theory. On that occasion, my funds were a long way from being unlimited but by my standards they were substantial and they had to be spent. The first hostelry I came across on my way into Siavonga was the Manchinchi Bay Lodge so I rode grandly in, airily greeted the astonished reception staff and made my way to the pool and luncheon area.

There was a conference or seminar in progress at the lodge and my sweat stained, travel-worn appearance hardly fitted in with the jackets, ties and neat safari suits of the delegates. I didn't care. I was almost home and for the next hour or so, I was rich. It was a heady feeling for a cycling tramp.

Sitting beside the swimming pool, I ordered lunch and a gin and tonic, taking care to ensure that the gin was of the imported variety. None of the local cooking poison for this wandering hedonist. From where I sat, I could look out across the lake to the brooding line of the Matusadona hills – a favourite haunt of mine and an area where my son Graeme plied his trade as a safari operator. I looked forward to paying him a visit.

Although the sun was every bit as hot as it had been on the road, it seemed somehow soothing now and I savoured the delicious feeling of being at ease in luxurious surroundings. This was the life and I was determined to enjoy it. On the other hand, it raised the question as to why I was subjecting my body to continual torment and existing in mobile squalor when I could be living comfortably like everyone else. It didn't make sense, even to me.

In my phone call to Missy from Riverside Mission, I had mentioned the approximate time of my arrival and although I was somewhat late, I knew they would be watching out for me at the dam wall, cameras poised and the welcome mat dusted off in readiness. Missy and daughter Deborah would have probably come up from Harare and they would all be there to greet me. I felt a glow of pleasurable, gin-inspired anticipation.

An excellent lunch and a couple more gins (imported of course) added to my sense of well being and as I cycled out of Manchinchi Bay I hardly noticed the stifling afternoon heat. It was a long climb back to the main road, but soon I was freewheeling down the hill toward the dam wall, the border posts and home. It was mid afternoon and I felt very pleased with myself.

The formalities on the Zambian side were haphazard and without strain, but the young immigration officer did his best to puncture my bubble of contentment.

"You will soon be back," he told me without emotion. "I don't know what is the matter with those fellows over there. Only last week they turned an American couple in a landrover back. They didn't have a return air ticket, even though they had their vehicle. Damned ridiculous hey?"

I agreed that it was but assured him that my case was different. I lived in Kariba so I would be all right. All the same, a worm of doubt wriggled in my vitals. Although I had spent most of my life in Zimbabwe and my children were still living there, I no longer held Zimbabwean nationality. Dual citizenship had been allowed when the country was Rhodesia, but with Independence, decisions had to be made. In my line of work, I am always likely to fall foul of over sensitive officialdom and in Africa, one needs a lifeline to use in times of trouble. British nationality has always been mine, so I renounced my Zimbabwean citizenship, but approaching Kariba, I suddenly wished I had one of those nice green Zimbabwean documents instead of my trusty British passport. I had been away from home for some considerable time and the Zimbabwean authorities are notoriously sticky with those who stay away for more than a year or two.

I pushed the doubts from my mind. I was going home. I was only minutes from seeing my family.

There was nobody to meet me on the wall. No family; no reporters; nobody to take a photograph. A group of South African tourists gazed somewhat incredulously at me and the lady of the party pulled her offspring anxiously into her bosom in case they contracted something unmentionable from the scruffy apparition on the yellow bicycle.

Stifling my disappointment at the lack of a reception, I pushed Harriet slowly up the hill to the familiar little border post. A novelty was the presence of a cholera desk, set up to prevent the disease coming down from Zambia, where it was said to be rife. I had seen no sign of it but at the request of the officer in attendance, I tipped my water supplies on to the ground, thereby severing my last link with Africa, north of the Zambezi. Water was no longer a problem in any case. I was back in civilisation. I could even use taps whenever I chose to. Freed from possible contamination, I propped Harriet against the side of the building and reported with my passport to Immigration Control.

An elderly official surveyed my documents with a sour expression. I was the only customer in the building and he had plenty of time to get me going and perhaps have some fun. I could feel my initial nervousness curdling into irritation as I waited. Sternly I instructed myself to remain calm.

"How long have you been out of the country?" The answer should have been obvious from my passport but I kept my cool.

"Three years."

He didn't comment and the room was silent as he turned back to my papers. A ceiling fan revolved arthritically and a gecko stalked a fly across a bare expanse of wall. Another fly, attracted by the sweaty haze around my head, spun into my cheek and I slapped it away.

"You will have to come in as a visitor and your resident status will be investigated in Harare," the officer told me eventually and I went back to fill in the form required by a visitor. This I duly represented and his eyes lit up in triumph.

"Where is your return air ticket?"

It was the question I had been dreading since my chat with the Zambian immigration official, but I forced myself to remain cool, calm and collected.

"I don't have one. I have my own transport."

I pointed to Harriet just outside the door and clearly visible from the desk. He shook his head in obvious exasperation.

"That is not transport. That is a bicycle."

I was sorely offended and Harriet seemed to slip a little against the door frame.

"I have travelled all the way from Nairobi on that bicycle."

He was unimpressed.

"Your return air ticket please."

I was so close to home. My children were only just down the road, yet this oaf was doing his best to ensure that I didn't see them. I asked for the officer in charge, hoping that it would be someone I knew. It wasn't and the argument went on.

"We cannot let you into the country without some indication that you will not be left for our government to support," the boss told me wearily. "The regulations insist that you have a return air ticket or sufficient funds with which to buy one."

"I do have sufficient finds," I protested, indicating the vastly inflated figure I had entered on my immigration form. He had seen it all before.

"Have you a credit card?" He asked and for a moment, I was stumped but only for a moment. Being of a profligate nature, I had never dared to avail myself of credit facilities but this obviously was not the time to admit it. I produced my visa debit card with an air of triumph. Other officials had gathered to watch the fun and the card was passed among them like a rare gem at an auction. Baffled looks were widespread and eventually the card was taken off to an inner sanctum for verification. The onlookers dispersed and I was left with the elderly one. We stared mutely at each other in ill concealed hostility.

After an absence of almost fifteen minutes, the officer in charge returned and held up my card.

"This is not for credit," he said accusingly. "How does it work?"

I improvised somewhat desperately.

"If I take it into a local bank," I told him desperately, "it takes but a telex or email to my own bank for me to be allowed a thousand pounds on the turn."

It sounded unlikely even to me and I don't think he was convinced. After a long moment of silent scrutiny, he sighed, handed the card back and waved me through with muttered instructions to his surly subordinate. Stamps descended upon my passport with unnecessary force and I moved across to the Customs desk where a young man lounged in his chair, a broad grin on his face.

"I suppose you are going to give me a hard time now," I muttered and his grin grew wider.

"Not at all Mr Lemon. You helped my father when I was a very young man and I am sure you are not going to smuggle anything in to the country – particularly on an *njinga*."

He laughed uproariously at his sally and although I couldn't remember him or his father, I joined in the merriment, even if it was at my expense.

Forty-five minutes after entering the building, I was out in the hot sunshine of Zimbabwe – the wanderer home after a long absence, my passport stamped and authority given for a one-month stay.

I was also very much alone.

<hr />

Moving slowly through the outskirts of Kariba, I reflected that my incredible luck was still with me. Ellen Butler would have said that it was the work of The Lord and perhaps it was. By rights, I should have been on my way back through Zambia, yet now it was merely a matter of cycling a few kilometres to Carribbea Bay and getting inside clean clothing and outside a gallon of tea.

For the moment, my problems were over and if there was still a long way to go – well, I was nearly half way with the easier half to come. I had been through a great deal and could surely take whatever was still in store for me. Tears welled in my eyes as I rode through the little town that I know so well.

Cycling through Mahombekombe Township, I was immediately struck by the contrast between local people and the friendly folk I had encountered north of the Zambezi. I was met with no shouts of encouragement from passers by. No youngsters ran beside me and those that looked up at my passing, quickly turned away again, obviously unimpressed and uninterested. An old friend passed me in his pick up truck and I waved unhappily, but he ignored me and trundled on. Kariba folk are accustomed to scruffy wanderers in their town and I suppose I looked like all the rest. I began to feel ever more despondent about my homecoming.

At Brian's front door, my daughter in law, Sarah was getting into her car. At the time she was running a catering business and was issuing instructions to her cook as I cycled up and stopped beside her. She glanced sideways but didn't pause in what she was saying. The cook stared at me with big round eyes. Even his obvious consternation was preferable to the general indifference with which I had been surrounded since returning home.

"Doesn't anyone want to know me in this benighted country?" I enquired plaintively and suddenly Sarah realised who I was.

"We didn't expect you until tomorrow," she explained a trifle defensively.

It was hardly the triumphant homecoming I had so eagerly anticipated.

PART TWO

South of the Zambezi

CHAPTER NINE

(Disappointment in Zimbabwe)

There is no hurry in Africa – how very true that is. Wanting to visit Graeme in his houseboat safari camp, I took the District Development Fund ferry across the lake and what should have been a five-hour journey took almost fourteen. We started out two and a half hours late in any case and one engine broke down half way across. The ferry was packed to the gunwales with people, chickens, baggage, crates of beer and an ancient land rover, but it wallowed and wobbled its way across a fortunately light swell. In spite of the delay nobody seemed in any way put out and Graeme met me in Bumi Harbour with the news that we were going to a bachelor party at Chalala Fishing Camp.

My life on the road was certainly proving full of variety.

He was a young bull and he knew that we were there. Only a thin strip of grey and tangled bush separated Graeme and I from the rhinoceros and he kept shuffling uncertainly towards us. I could smell his musty scent and his great wet sniffs seemed to reverberate through the bush around us. Even the birds were quiet in their absorption with the drama and from where I stood, the bull looked awfully big.

Graeme and I were enjoying an impromptu foot safari in the Matusadona National Park and I wasn't missing Harriet at all. She was back in Kariba and it felt good to feel hard ground beneath my feet and allow my legs to stretch to their fullest extent. It also felt good to be in a truly wild place again, surrounded by dangerous wild life and enjoying every exciting moment.

As the rhino shuffled closer, I struggled to focus my camera but the automatic setting could not differentiate between the colour of the intervening foliage and that of the animal. I could feel the tension in my son as he waited for an opportunity to withdraw, but I was in no hurry to move away. On the last occasion, we had walked together in the bush, I carried the rifle and pointed out items of interest while he trotted at my heels. Now the positions were reversed and Graeme carried the big .458 across his chest, while I struggled with my recalcitrant camera.

Eventually after my slightly anxious son had talked quietly to the great animal, imploring it to go away and leave us alone, the rhino gave a final indignant snort and trippled away through the scrub, leaving me frustrated at not getting my photograph and Graeme relieved that the encounter had ended without mishap.

We chatted about it afterwards and I had to agree that it might well have proved a dangerous moment, yet I had not been as nervous with that rhinoceros as I had with the various uniformed officials I had encountered along the way. After a lifetime in the bush, I felt I could understand the great beast while the officialdom of Africa was an unknown and very volatile quantity. I had been incredibly lucky with my border crossings, but I was at the stage when my heart beat faster whenever I found myself approaching anyone in uniform. Policemen, immigration officers, customs officials – they all held tremendous power and any one of them could end my entire trip if he or she felt like it or if I offended them in any way.

It wasn't that they were necessarily vindictive, but I knew from my own experience with the Zimbabwe Republic Police that training in public relations was no longer part of government curricula. Few of them had been taught how to deal with people like me, yet their position was all powerful and I was entirely at their mercy.

We saw other animals and had a close up encounter with lions during those idyllic few days and when I flew back across the lake in a light aircraft, I looked down and wondered whether I would ever see my favourite lake again and for how long it would retain its magical ambience.

For it is a fact that the encroachment of Mankind is ruining the ecological balance of Africa and nowhere was this more apparent than in my own country. At the time of my cycle ride, the Department of National Parks & Wild Life Management were doing their best to halt the rapid decline in animal populations, but they were fighting a losing battle. The trouble was that due to years of government mismanagement, ordinary people were starving and the department was under funded and ill equipped. So-called war veterans had already begun ravaging the land with vicious occupations and takeovers of prosperous farms and the battle against rampant poaching was inevitably going to be a losing one. Since then, the situation has deteriorated further and the wild life of Zimbabwe is in danger of being decimated.

Conservation bodies were and still are trying to assist from abroad, but their efforts are planned from the sanctuary of overseas headquarters and were rarely proving workable when put into practice. Few of these overseas conservationists ever visit the wild places of Africa and consequently have only a vague idea of the mass tragedy that is unfolding with the wild life.

Yet Zimbabwe is still one of the last great strongholds of exotic African animals and I had always considered myself rarely privileged to have been allowed so much time in Kariba and the Zambezi Valley – surely the most enchanted area of the country.

And for all the disappointment of my arrival, I had enjoyed my few days in Kariba. I met up with many old friends, ate well, drank well and felt stronger and fitter than I had in many a long year. It felt marvellous to sleep in comfort and enjoy three square meals a day, while I thrived on the attention I was getting from people anxious to hear about my adventure. One old friend did his best to puncture my bubble of newly found self-confidence however.

Big Anthony Harvey – 'Harvs' to his friends and his lovely wife Sue – was a local businessman and when we met up one morning, he questioned me closely about my trip.

"I suppose you are quite pleased with yourself, Dave Lemon?"

All Davids grow accustomed to the cutting down of their name but I don't suppose many of them approve.

Nevertheless, I agreed that I was 'quite pleased' with my performance so far.

"Well," Harvey had a sly gleam in his eye and I wondered what was coming. "I picked up a bloke the other day who had not only cycled from Cairo to Cape Town but was on his way back."

I allowed that this was no mean feat. After all, I could afford to be magnanimous as there were few long distance cyclists on the road in Africa who were as old as I was. I could let the youngsters have their fun.

"Not only that," Harvs tightened the screw, "but this bloke was in his seventies."

There was little I could say to that so we went off for a beer. Some people never grow up.

I was still smiling about that conversation when I rode on toward Makuti and civilisation a few days later. Ungainly looking hornbills swooped from tree to tree in front of me while an old bull elephant watched me morosely from the side of the road. When he was satisfied that I posed no threat, he swung his head so that his ears made a sound like a pistol shot before resuming his leisurely foraging. His tusks were old, cracked and yellow while his stomach swung ponderously as he moved. A vulture eyed me from a treetop and leaving Harriet in the road, I walked across to investigate. A well-eaten buffalo carcass served as a grisly reminder that lions were about and it behoved me to be careful.

For hours, I felt that I was alone in the world apart from sable antelope with their huge, swinging horns, warthog, buffalo, massively-built eland and a host of smaller animals that watched me from the side of the road on my leisurely ride through the hills. Twenty kilometres from Makuti, I spotted a pack of about fifteen wild dogs and that was a wonderful moment. More properly known as *lycaon pictus* or the painted hunting dog, these animals are not even part of the dog family, but they have been almost wiped out in Africa and to see so many of them together was a huge privilege. Only a kilometre further on, I was even more fortunate to see a big male leopard sliding frantically down the bole of a tree. Once on the ground, he turned and glared at me, those cold yellow eyes sending a distinct shiver through my soul. These beautiful cats are also under threat and I felt very much part of the bush around me as the magnificent spotted killer stalked regally away.

I camped beneath the stars and lost myself in the magnificence of the African night. I heard the sobbing cough of lions, the rasp of a hunting leopard and the varying calls of hyena, distant hippopotamus and jackal. It all sounds pretty noisy when written down, but the sounds blended into so harmonious a chorus that they filled my soul with peace. The gentle flame of a mopani fire fuelled my dreams and I felt glad to be alive and part of Africa.

During the day, the going was hard and hot but I was in no hurry and moved along at a delicious dawdle, drinking in the sights, sounds and smells of my wild homeland. Can there be anything more spiritually humbling than to wallow in the colours of a bushveld dawn, breathe in hot dust at midday or dream to the fragrance of burning mopani logs as the sun goes down. I had it all and when I reached the outskirts of the Karoi farming area, I felt a sense of deep disappointment that the Zambezi Valley was irrevocably behind me and I was unlikely to see much more wild life in the course of my journey.

In Chinhoyi I spent half an hour in earnest conversation with a man who had lost both legs to a land mine blast during the bush war. He moved about on a small, skateboard-like trolley and seemed quite content with his lot, although I was glad to be on Harriet rather than his flimsy little conveyance.

"I work as a clerk," Daniel Murape told me cheerfully and it turned out that he was employed by a local supermarket and made a comparatively decent living. He offered me accommodation for the night but I declined on the grounds that I wanted to reach Harare as soon as possible. Cycling on, I couldn't help the uncomfortable feeling that it was Daniel's disability rather than my need for haste that had made me decline the offer. My own fitness and ability to cycle long distances might well have embarrassed me in the sanctuary of his home. Why is it that those of us fortunate enough to have intact bodies find it awkward to deal with those who haven't?

It took me four days to reach Harare and once there, I lost myself in idleness once more. It was wonderful to have time on my hands – time to wander the tree-lined avenues, visit friends or tinker with my bicycle. Mind you, this last enterprise might have had catastrophic consequences had not Lemon's Luck been riding on my shoulder yet again.

Before leaving England, I had received detailed instruction on removing the wheel bearings for servicing and I thought I knew exactly what to do. Everything seemed to be going well but when I triumphantly withdrew the hub, a cascade of ball bearings erupted, to shoot off in every direction. I replaced them individually with tweezers and then repeated the whole disastrous process with the other wheel. I was almost reduced to impotent tears and it was only when I reassembled the bike that I remembered a tool I had brought with me, specifically designed to remove wheel hubs without incident.

Many months later it remained unused in my kit.

Harare itself was disappointing. A beautifully designed city, it has always been one of the jewels of Africa but decay had begun to set in. The avenues were as beautiful as ever, but the city centre was a mess. Litter bins were filled to overflowing, long queues snaked around every corner and beggars wailed their entreaties from every vantage point. Crime seemed out of control and the police appeared powerless to do anything but beat up political enemies of Robert Mugabe. Lack of transport was the usual excuse for lack of police action but during my stay, the constabulary took over an hour to attend a mystery blast at the Sheraton Hotel, even though the central police station was only a ten-minute walk away.

Traffic conditions in and around the city were chaotic, with scant regard paid for regulations, driving manners or traffic lights – robots as they are known throughout Southern Africa. I spoke to one young woman who having failed her driving test on four occasions, resorted to bribery in order to avoid a repeat performance.

"I just handed over a great big parcel of cash to the examiner," she told me simply. "He wrote out the form and I became a licensed driver. It was simple really."

Simple perhaps, but hardly conducive to keeping death off the roads.

One morning I was cycling slowly through The Avenues, meditating on my trip and enjoying the sunshine when I found myself being accosted by two soldiers – their AK47 rifles pointed menacingly at my chest. Quite unwittingly, I had strayed behind the residence of President Mugabe – 'Comrade Bob' as he is known to most of his subjects. I was on a public road and minding my own business, but such is the paranoia of Africa and the power of he-who-wields-the-kalashnikov that I was lucky not to get myself shot. Other innocents had not been as fortunate.

But the weather was benign, I had time on my hands and I was enjoying myself in the city of my youth. The days passed all too quickly and soon it was time to be back on the road.

I left Harare in a pall of smog that had enveloped the city for the previous three days. As I cycled out along the Bulawayo Road, it hung in the air behind me like a great grey sponge. It is another sad reflection on our automated world that air pollution is becoming a problem even in the highlands of Central Africa.

Bystanders stared unemotionally at me as I cycled past. A vendor of fishing worms muttered a laconic greeting, but in general I was ignored. This was disconcerting after the enthusiastic reaction Harriet and I had provoked in other parts of Africa, but it seemed symptomatic of the general malaise that was gripping the Zimbabwean people. They appeared cowed and frightened for their future, which left little room for curiosity about the motives of a cycling stranger. There was neither friendliness nor unfriendliness in their stares, merely a blank acceptance of my presence on a heavily laden bicycle. It was as though everyone was accustomed to such sights and had grown tired of them. I was not even worth a second glance. I wondered somewhat sourly what had happened to the innate friendliness that has always been a trait of my fellow countrymen.

Another anomaly of independent Africa soon came into view and added to my developing depression. Nestling among the high-density townships and tumble-down squatter camps were twin concrete monoliths on opposite sides of the road.

It seems to be accepted that every independent country in Africa should have its own national sports stadium, built to Olympic standards and more ornate than the stadia belonging to neighbouring states. I saw them throughout my journey and never ceased to marvel at their magnificent impracticality. Harare already possessed two fine sports arenas prior to Independence, but their latest expensive monstrosity beamed down on me as I cycled slowly out of the city. Built by the Chinese in return for future favours, it looked for all the world like a bloated Buddha, wondering what on earth I was doing cycling past on a yellow bicycle. The stadium aroused considerable ire among Zimbabweans at the time of building and has never had adequate usage – Zim being far too insignificant a sporting nation for that.

A slightly more understandable edifice was Heroes Acre on the opposite side of the road and a few kilometres further on. Armed gate guards glowered at my passing but I was allowed to ride on unmolested, even though I couldn't help wondering why that particular monument to the fallen should be constructed so that it put all similar memorials to shame. I am all for honouring those who gave their lives for freedom, but even the fallen heroes themselves must feel a little abashed to find themselves interred behind towering portals of black marble. Ironically, a few thousand of those they gave their lives for were crowded together in obvious degradation less than a kilometre away.

Shaking my head, I tried to banish my ready cynicism and ignore the world around me. Putting my head down, I pedalled on for Bulawayo.

Because really, my stay in Harare had been most enjoyable. Apart from family and friends, I had met with a bewildering variety of people, all anxious to hear tales of my trip. I had chatted with farmers, hoteliers, peasants and politicians, as well as an assistant commissioner of police and a retired general. In addition to my Matusadona safari, I had played golf in the mountains with Brian, attended a society wedding with Missy and Deborah and been an interested – if not particularly impressed – participant in a writers' workshop at the Harare International Book Fair. It had all been great fun but there was an underlying worry about the future among Zimbabweans that disturbed me. Robert Mugabe seemed somehow to have cowed a once spirited nation into humble acceptance of their lot.

This was borne out by the very first encounter I had along the road to Bulawayo.

Gilbert Nyandoro was a former police colleague of mine and we had been through a lot together in those heady days before Rhodesia became Zimbabwe. We met by chance at a roadside kiosk where I stopped for a coke and he told me that he was running a smallholding in the Mhondoro Communal Land.

"I am one of the lucky ones," Gilbert told me sadly. "I have a little money, my land and a few *mombies* for my old age. I grow *mealies* and watch the world go by while I dream about the good old days. Others are not so fortunate. They have no money and food is becoming increasingly scarce.

'Prices keep rising in the stores and many basic food-stuffs are impossible to find. There is mass unemployment and much starvation throughout the country.

'It will get worse," he added forebodingly and shook his head at my obvious question.

"What can we do? This is our government and Mugabe will never allow himself to be defeated in an election. The situation will deteriorate even further until we have another civil war. Already the young men are spoiling for a fight, but they have no weapons and both the army and the police are behind Mugabe, although there is increasing dissatisfaction in the lower ranks."

Passing through the tiny farming hamlet of Selous, I called into the ramshackle local hotel where I witnessed an example of this general discontent for myself. I needed a beer and in the gloomy bar, fell into conversation with a group of youngsters, all of whom professed to be unemployed, broke and wondering what to do with their lives.

"We have no future," one young man told me. "It is alright for the president. He has his cars and his mansions but we are hungry now. It is time for the Old Man to go and let someone else run the country."

When I gently pointed out that he would have a chance to unseat Mugabe at the next election, he and his friends were openly scornful.

"That cannot happen," another youth muttered. "He will rig the voting so that he stays in power. The only way for him to lose is if he dies."

While we were talking, a tall man in a suit and wearing dark glasses came into the bar and the youths who had been so animated only moments before, broke off their conversation with me and paid close attention to their beers. The stranger looked me over and then moved across to join me.

"Why are you here?" he demanded. "What are you doing in this bar?"

"I am thirsty and called in for a beer," I told him politely. "Is there a law against that?"

"You are here to cause trouble," he accused and I noticed that those who had been so animated a few minutes previously were quietly ebbing from the bar, leaving me alone with the stranger and a couple of obvious thugs who had come in with him. Even the barman had disappeared.

"I am a traveller heading for Bulawayo," I told him wearily. "I do not want to cause trouble and was enjoying a simple conversation with those young men until you came in."

"Do not talk to me like that," he snapped. "You must show me respect. Just because you are white, it does not mean you are better than me."

"I am considerably older than you," I pointed out. "I thought African culture demanded respect for one's elders?"

For some reason, that seemed to floor him and swallowing his beer, he muttered something to his companions and stalked out of the bar, leaving me shaky with reaction. I had encountered so little racism on my journey down Africa and that little diatribe left a nasty taste in my mouth. Blinking against the sunshine after the gloom inside the bar, I climbed back on Harriet and cycled sadly down the road. What was happening to my beloved country?

A couple of kilometres out of town, a small group of men emerged from the bush and I tensed myself for another confrontation., I need not have worried, as it was the young men I had been talking to in the hotel bar. They looked nervously up and down before coming across to where I had stopped.

"We have to be careful nowadays," their spokesman told me. "The CIOs (members of the Central Intelligence Organisation) are everywhere and if that man had heard what we were saying, we would have been locked up and probably beaten."

We chatted for a while and then they waved me on my way. I was encouraged by their attitude, but with hindsight, they were right about Mugabe and elections. Not so very many years later, Zimbabwe is in ruins and so many people have been beaten, raped and murdered by Mugabe's thugs that I can only wonder what happened to those young men in Selous. I just hope they survived the troubles.

I was to hear similar talk of hopelessness and insurrection throughout Matabeleland, but it has all come to nothing and nobody knows what will eventually happen to my country or its people. I rode into that vast, rugged province feeling very despondent but hoping that life would seem better in Bulawayo. I have always loved the city and visiting it again had been a major factor in my decision to take a thousand kilometre detour through Botswana rather than heading straight for the South African border at Beit Bridge.

I was buffeted by crosswinds through the bleak Midlands plains and suffered two punctures in quick succession near Gweru. A passing lorry driver stopped to lend a hand, advancing the theory that many punctures are caused by the afternoon heat of the tarmac. It certainly seemed feasible as I was seldom able to find any particular reason for my tubes being holed.

Below the great clock tower in the centre of Gweru, I stopped to allow a pretty young mum across the road with her pushchair and she gave me such a lovely smile that my spirits instantly lifted. After all, I was back on the road, free to do exactly as I wanted and an object of envy to all those luckless citizens, condemned to live out their lives in servitude to the system. I was a lucky man and had no reason for my despondency.

"Thank you Ma'am," I tipped my hat to the lovely young mum and rode on, leaving her looking after me with a slightly quizzical expression. She probably still wonders what she did to gain my gratitude, but if she ever reads this narrative – 'Ma'am, your smile made my day.'

I spent one uncomfortable night fighting an icy gale on the Somabula Flats and suffered a minor fall near Shangani, but at last I saw the skyline of Bulawayo ahead of me. It was with a feeling of coming home that I finally rode into the city.

In spite of its turbulent past, Bulawayo (The Place of Killing) is everything an African city ought to be. The buildings are modern without being ostentatious and the streets have retained their original width. They were designed to allow a full span of sixteen trek oxen to turn around and the extra space is now taken up with centre street parking. An easy pace of life and a wonderful climate make this a marvellous place to be.

'In Bulawayo, the skies are bluer and the smiles are wider,' say the locals and I cannot help but agree.

Yet I also have some horrific memories of this dusty city. In the early eighties, I was a Troop Commander in the police Support Unit. This was the fighting arm of the police force and I led the men of Charlie Troop into battle through the townships of Entumbane, Luveve, Ntabazinduna and others. Our enemy at the time were bored former guerrillas of both Mugabe and Joshua Nkomo, intent on violence and not caring whether they fought each other, us, or the two mainly black, army companies that were also brought in to quell the situation. Over two separate spells of three days, I was shot at, rocketed and generally insulted by guerrillas and civilians alike. It was horrific and very frightening, but when it was all over and the city resumed its peaceful mien, it almost seemed as though nothing had happened.

But such is the way of Africa and it is never more apparent than in this original city of the Matabele kings. Only a few kilometres out of town are the magical Matobo hills. In these ruggedly magnificent ramparts of granite lie the remains of Cecil Rhodes and other heroes of the pioneer age. The hills are also the spiritual home of the Matabele people and even to a hard-headed cynic like myself, there are strange forces wandering among the rocks in this enchanted range. Many of the Matabele warriors and their chiefs are also buried here and I cannot think of a finer place for any man to spend the long eternity.

Leaving Harriet with friends to have solid inner tubes fitted, I took myself off to the Matopos for a few days of solitary meditation. I needed to be truly alone – to find myself again and shake off the depression that was beginning to envelop me and sour my enjoyment of the trip. I slept in caves and tramped the rocky slopes, enjoying the crystal clarity of the air and beginning to feel better by the moment. Perhaps the best way to describe my sojourn in those magical hills is to quote directly from my journal.

3rd September

'*Words are somehow inadequate,*' I wrote, '*to describe the lonely serenity of these hills. As I sit alone in the biting cold of the mountain air, vast grey ramparts of rock extend in every direction like the petrified waves of a forgotten ocean. I can see a tiny spot that is a black eagle soaring in the blue vastness overhead but otherwise I might as well be alone in the world. The silence is absolute and the loneliness somehow uplifting. The true Spirits of Africa are all around me.*'

I prayed a great deal in the Matopos and didn't confine my prayers to the Christian Deity I was brought up to worship. One cold morning, I visited the shrine of the Matabele weather spirit, Willelane, where I handed over a few dollars and asked for good weather on the rest of my trip. I obviously didn't contribute enough though as it was not to be and I had a great deal of bad weather to endure in the weeks ahead. I didn't know that at the time however and my break from the usual cycling routine certainly made me feel considerably better. The rocky hills of the Matopos are a place where local people pay homage to a variety of Spirits apart from Willelane and I invoked them all, to ask their collective blessing on my enterprise, my future, my family and friends – even my trusty bicycle. When I returned to Bulawayo, I felt refreshed and ready for anything that the road could throw at me.

On the morning I left the city, I was saddened to see that smog was evident, even there. It was not as dense as it had been in Harare, but it was easily seen and I railed against the depredations of modern society as I rode out of town.

It was a very hot hundred kilometres to Plumtree and in spite of an early start, I made slow progress, arriving in the little border town late in the afternoon. A friendly clerk in the post office handed over a package of letters from England and explained without embarrassment how he had been looking forward to reading them had I not turned up. I called at the local hotel for tea and a wash, only to find that the whole town was out of water. I did get my tea eventually but arrived at the border with Botswana hot, red-faced and sweating.

I had financed my way through Zimbabwe by working exchange deals with friends, so was a little nervous when I presented myself at the Customs desk. I had the same amount of cash and travellers' cheques on me as I had brought into the country and like a fool, I had honestly answered all the questions on the visitors' entry form. How would I now explain the fact that I had spent nearly three weeks in Zimbabwe without spending any money?

I need not have worried. A bored looking lady stamped my forms without even glancing at them and I was through to my fifth African country with a minimum of hassle.

For the first time in my life I was not sorry to be leaving Zimbabwe. I have lived there for most of my life and love the place with the passion that any man reserves for his homeland. I fought a bitter war for what I believed was right in the country and stayed on at the conclusion of that war, determined not to run away from the inevitable problems of transition. It was only a need to escape from the pains of divorce and separation from my children that drove me away and I pray that – notwithstanding my somewhat acerbic comments in this narrative – I will eventually end my days in my beloved country.

But things had changed for Zimbabwe and its people. I was saddened by the degeneration that had taken place in the years of my absence. The country was rapidly sliding downhill toward inevitable chaos and the people – who have always been more resilient than most – seemed to have lost their collective spirit. Robert Mugabe and his sycophantic thugs were exerting a stranglehold on the nation and even though thousands were starving, nobody showed any desire to fight back.

Nor were the rest of the world prepared to help in ousting Mugabe and his evil regime and as I rode into Botswana, I could only wonder what further horrors lay in wait for my countrymen.

CHAPTER TEN

(Hard and Boring Days)

In 1963, the Rendle family and I had driven from
Bulawayo through to Beit Bridge and then on into South
Africa, but Harriet and I had taken a different route
through Zimbabwe. Quite apart from my desire to spend
time in Bulawayo, my decision to detour through
Botswana was inspired by a short visit I paid to that
country in the early nineties. I had enjoyed the vast landscape and friendly people to such an extent that I was
determined to return and see it from grass roots level
once again. My cycle trip provided me with the opportunity, and the extra distance involved didn't really
matter. I was not in any hurry to reach Cape Town.

There were many occasions during my first week or
so in the country when I seriously doubted the wisdom
of my decision. I certainly did not enjoy the six hundred-
kilometre section between Plumtree and Gaborone. The
few people I met along the way were friendly enough and
my daily progress was well up to the hundred kilometre
mark, but the road was flat and straight, the countryside
dry, brown and dusty and the heat utterly devastating.
When I removed my shirt at night, it crackled with caked
salt and I drank copious quantities of brackish water as

I rode along. At night, the temperature plummeted and I woke in the mornings to find my bedding soaked with dew and my bones aching from the cold.

It was on this section that Harriet showed her first signs of temperament and I couldn't really blame her. She had taken far more punishment than I had and apart from puncturing her tyres when she needed a rest, had never made any protest. She was probably in marginally better shape than I was, but one evening I casually fingered the front wheel to discover that a number of spokes were very loose indeed. There had been strange clanking noises emanating from that area for some time but I had put them down to fair wear and tear, so worried not. Now I berated myself for my stupidity. In the dim light of my torch I worked on that wheel with the spoke key but there were four spokes that resolutely refused to go back into place. This was disturbing but I decided that it was not too serious. We had coped with worse. Nevertheless, I kept a careful eye on that wheel over succeeding weeks and whenever it began to wobble more than was its wont, I did what I could with the spoke key. In this manner we shuddered and clanked our way southward.

I entered Botswana on a Friday afternoon and the first major problem I encountered was not Harriet, but a lack of the local currency. On my previous visit, South African rands had been readily interchangeable with the Botswana pula, but with the steady devaluation of the rand this was no longer the case. I hadn't thought to buy pula in Zimbabwe and the first Botswana banks I would come to were in Francistown, which I wouldn't reach until well into Saturday afternoon when they would be closed. With no money and very little food, it looked like being a very long weekend.

By Sunday morning I was hungry and when I was hailed by a group of local men outside a roadside tavern, I was only too pleased to stop for a chat. I was hoping that someone might have been able to change a few of my rands, so that I could at least buy myself a cup of tea. In the event, I was asked inside and before I knew what was happening, tea and a plate of maize meal (*pollichi* in Botswana) with goat stew were placed in front of me. At my protest, I was advised by Andrew Marridi, a local schoolteacher that the meal was on the house.

"It is our custom," he told me, "that when a stranger appears in our midst, he is fed before we eat ourselves."

I was somewhat lost for words at this unexpected generosity, but anxious not to offend against local etiquette, tucked in with a hearty appetite. The stew was delicious and brought life back to flagging muscles. Afterwards, I enjoyed a long chat with Andrew and his cronies and when I rode on, their good wishes rang in my ears while my heart sang with the joys of travel in rural Africa.

Stories of travellers dying of thirst in Botswana are legion and water had always been my greatest worry. In Bulawayo I had been warned that the entire region was in the grip of a ferocious drought and advised to forget all about Botswana and take the shortest route through to South Africa. This would have meant cutting back through Beit Bridge but it did not appeal and once I was on the road to Plumtree, I was committed.

I had managed to get hold of a number of plastic containers for my water and these I carried in my panniers. After leaving Bulawayo, they seemed subject to some malevolent fate. Perhaps the *tokoloshe* was at

work. He is regarded as a malicious spirit throughout
Africa and while he seemed to have treated me quite
kindly for most of the way, he was always likely to get
me into trouble. Whatever the case, I suffered a series of
mishaps and my water supply diminished with frightening rapidity. I dropped and split one bottle near Figtree
and another one mysteriously disappeared in Francistown. A third broke on the way in to Serule, but the
biggest disaster of all occurred when my canvas water
bag sprung a leak forty kilometres north of Mahalapye.
Dry, frightening countryside spread away around me,
the occasional pile of bleached bones testifying to the
harshness of the environment. I was close to tears as
I tried to stop the water spurting from the side of my
precious water bag. I had bought it in Nairobi and although evaporation and seepage meant that I did not
get the full benefit of its three and a half litre capacity,
the fact that the water was always icily cold more than
made up for any deficiency.

My thoughts as I sat beside the road with the ruined
bag were beyond description. I was shattered and did not
see how I could possibly go on. Nor could I stay where I
was. A long way from anywhere in one of the hottest and
least hospitable corners of Africa, I was very close to
panic. The bottles fitted to Harriet contained a scant litre
and a half, while another plastic-contained litre was
hidden somewhere in a pannier. Even with careful
husbanding, this could not possibly last me through the
day, let along however long it might take me to reach the
ever-so-distant sanctuary of Gaborone.

But the *tokoloshe* had tired of his mischievous goad-
ing. Either that or he had been overruled by a more
benevolent Being. Ten kilometres after the bag had split

and moments before my heart was likely to break, I rode up to a veterinary checkpoint. They were searching vehicles for anything likely to assist the spread of foot and mouth disease. I wasn't a problem in that regard and was invited back to their camp for a cup of tea. There, I was not only able to slake my burgeoning thirst, but also buy another canvas water bag that by almost unbelievable coincidence, was hanging unused in a tree. These bags are seldom seen nowadays and from the markings on its canvas, this one had been filched from a Maun-based safari company, but I didn't care. The bag held five litres and was exactly what I needed so I was happy to part with a precious twenty-rand note. That was half what I had paid in Nairobi but the chap who sold it to me was also well pleased with the transaction – probably relieved to be free of such incriminating evidence of his treachery to former employers.

Riding on, I offered fervent thanks to God, to the *tokoloshe* and to whatever other Deities were keeping such a benevolent eye on my progress. I had water again so I would survive after all.

If heat and the lack of water were my major problems in Botswana, boredom ran them a close second. The countryside was so flat, so unchanging, so utterly drab and uninteresting. Vast expanses of mopani forest stretched away around me, and my days degenerated into a painful, sweaty process of pushing pedals and fighting to keep sweat out of my eyes. When I found a modicum of shade, I would stop for a long midday siesta, but it was too hot for proper rest and I would cycle on, unrefreshed and irritable. Between Serule and Mahalapye I passed through a wide belt of scrub where horse flies added their stinging assaults to the misery of the moment, and I cursed myself for choosing this inhospitable route when I could have been enjoying far pleasanter conditions on the cool slopes of the South African Zoutpansberg. At that stage the upper precipices of Mount Everest seemed infinitely preferable to the monotonous torture of Botswana – even with a bicycle.

Solid inner tubes made pedalling even more of a strain and I could see that my tyres were wearing away with alarming rapidity. The new set up did at least allow me to move well away from the road at night without worrying about punctures however and most of my Botswana camps were in delightful surroundings, spoiled only marginally by a total absence of water. One evening I awoke to a deep sobbing sound that seemed to shake the trees around me and burgeoning nervousness kept me awake for much of the night. Lions are prevalent – and notorious for their man eating propensities – in Botswana, and although I had never heard of them being encountered in that particular region, I did not want to end up as dinner for a hungry cat. It turned out to be a very long night.

I had intended an overnight stop in Mahalapye, the approximate half way point on this section but the town was a disappointment. At the Mahalapye Hotel, the receptionist kept me waiting for nearly ten minutes while she giggled and crooned into the telephone and then refused to accept travellers' cheques. I could have changed them at a nearby bank, but I was angered by her attitude and cycled on to sleep in the bush.

Nearing Gaborone, my front wheel wobbled ever more alarmingly, a thorn in my finger turned septic and

I gashed my thumb while slicing *biltong* with my bush knife. I was a mess but consoled myself with the thought within a week, I would be with my sister in Johannesburg, cold beer to hand and the delights of a swimming pool ever available. While I was engaged in such happy reveries, a bus passed so close to me that I was blown right off my bike and landed in an angrily shouting heap on the verge of the road. Fortunately it was soft sand so only my pride was hurt.

I passed the occasional lonely kraal during those long, empty days and at one of them I took a tentative sip of *kali,* the local home brew. The word means 'cheeky' in *Swahili* and the potion had all the beneficial effects of a kick in the head from an angry buffalo. I was grateful for the water provided to take the sting away and my teeth had a definite itch for some hours after that little experiment.

At another kraal a couple of days later, I set my camera up to photograph four of us seated outside a hut and the old gentleman who owned the place suddenly burst into explosive laughter.

"What's the matter?" I enquired when he finally subsided into teary spluttering.

"Anybody seeing that picture," he explained between further bursts of merriment, "will think you have a black wife. Look…"

He pointed out that the four of us were sitting in a line. He beside his wife and me paired with the comeliest of his daughters. I protested that she was too pretty – and far too young – for me and when the photograph was developed, I sent him a copy, inscribed with suitable comment. I only hope the lady was not offended.

CHAPTER ELEVEN

(Franz from Austria)

Of all the characters I met in my months on the road, perhaps the most fascinating was Franz Madl. His was the sort of larger than life personality that would not seem out of place in the pages of Rider Haggard or the incomparable John Buchan. The impression he gave of wild eccentricity was heightened by two yellow dogs that frolicked at his heels.

Tall, loose-limbed and tanned to the consistency of fine old leather, Franz fell into step beside me as I was crossing the main square in Gaborone. At the time I was replete and well satisfied at reaching the Botswana capital. I had shared coffee and toast at the Catholic seminary with Sister Zora, a charming nun from Slovenia who had given me further insight into the torments besetting exiles from strife-torn Yugoslavia. In spite of her worries, the kindly Sister had treated me right royally and even allowed me to shower and shave in the bathroom reserved for visiting bishops. Now I had merely to change a travellers' cheque and I could relax for a day or two in congenial surroundings. My troubles were forgotten and I was totally content.

"Marvellous way to travel," Franz commented as he strode along beside me. I agreed non-committally and he stuck out a hand in greeting.

"Franz from Austria," he introduced himself and I'm afraid I couldn't resist the obvious riposte.

"David from Zimbabwe."

The formalities over, he suggested tea and a short while later I found myself at a terrace table overlooking the square. Harriet had been left in the dubious care of a street vendor and Franz was holding court like a visiting potentate.

But that was the way of the man. He descended upon that particular hotel like a whirlwind, much to the amusement of the staff who obviously knew him well. Sweeping into the foyer, he demanded – and received – mail from the reception desk, greeted everyone by name and made his way up the stairs like a destroyer scything its way through a sea of grinning bell boys, waiters and assorted hotel staff. Feeling conspicuously scruffy in such opulent surroundings, I trailed in his wake, followed in turn by the dogs, their tails vibrating ecstatically at the variety of smells laid on by the management for their benefit.

"Kalahari lions," Franz had already explained his canine escorts. "They follow me everywhere and are not used to the city."

This was completely untrue but it took me a long time to discover that the dogs didn't even belong to Franz. In the meantime, although lovable beasts, they proved an absolute nuisance and created havoc wherever we went. Franz seemed unabashed by the chaos.

We were approached by a number of supplicants while we sat on that terrace and I was introduced to them all as 'David – my Zimbabwean friend who writes books and rides bicycles.' Franz appeared to conduct a number of minor business meetings and I grew quite bewildered, trying to figure out what he did for a living. Whenever I asked, he adroitly evaded the issue.

"I am a professional holidaymaker," he told me at one stage. "I live in the Kalahari where I don't have to worry about people and I make lots of money. I have wild animals all around me and my only companions are the Bushmen. In the desert, life is free."

My sentiments exactly but being the cynical soul that I am, I was not sure what to believe among Franz' fund of stories. I was to discover that the more outlandish the tale, the more likely it was to be true, while in more mundane matters such as the dogs, he allowed free rein to his imagination.

An incredibly complex character was Franz Madl. He had lived in Botswana for many years and spoke the Tswana language like a native, even though his English had a heavy, European bias. He seemed to have friends in all sectors of society and while he did indeed prospect for diamonds in the Kalahari from time to time, he proved to be a wheeler/dealer of some magnitude. He used the plusher hotels of Gaborone as his offices, availing himself of their secretarial facilities and using the telephone and telex machines to contact people in a variety of countries.

"The hotels have everything I need," he told me. "They type up my documents and provide a suitable setting for meetings with clients. I can always get coffee or a meal and don't have the expense of renting a city office that I don't need."

It seemed an estimable arrangement to me and Franz was certainly greeted with enthusiasm in all the local hostelries. On learning that I was a stranger to Gaborone, he appointed himself my mentor and – dogs in tow – took me to see the sights.

"Stay a few days," he offered. "You cannot be in a hurry and I will show you all there is to see. You can even come back to my camp in the Kalahari when I return in a day or two."

That was an offer I could not have refused. The Kalahari is one part of Africa I have only read about and the prospect of those vast, trackless wastes, abundant wild life and cold desert stars was an overwhelming inducement to tarry awhile.

Franz' truck was apparently undergoing repairs, but he cheerfully importuned a replacement from a local diamond prospecting company where the American manager appeared only too willing to hand over the keys.

"They owe me a favour," Franz told me smugly, but I don't think it was that. Perhaps it was the sheer, overwhelming personality of the man. He was completely at ease wherever we went and in most establishments we visited, he seemed to have his personal bottle of wine tucked away somewhere, to be smilingly produced as soon as he came into view.

A smash hit with the women too was our Franz. In one shopping arcade, he purchased a bunch of red roses and handed out individual blooms to various ladies of his acquaintance and probably a number that he didn't know. These ranged from the hard-faced proprietor of a Chinese restaurant to a young black girl, forlornly sweeping out a shop doorway. They all greeted his largesse with appreciative squeals and I could only shake my head in envious bemusement.

During the next two and a half days, we visited hotels, beer halls, restaurants and private homes. We drank beer, wine and tea in copious quantities and our meals ranged from an excellent breakfast at the Gaborone Sun to a greasy hamburger in the Sunrise Café and *frikadelln* with German friends. We spent one night in the empty dormitory of a Cheshire home for the disabled and another on top of a small *kopje*, from where we watched the sun rise over Gaborone.

I listened in mute amazement as he knowledgeably discussed import permits, tax problems and the intricacies of international finance with assorted business cronies and on one memorable occasion, I kept a suitably legal silence as he negotiated the purchase of a light aircraft, computer equipment and three land rovers with a bevy of South African businessmen.

"I don't entirely trust these fellows and need them to think I have my lawyer present," he explained prior to the meeting, which was to be held in the plush surroundings of the Sheraton Hotel. "With your police background, you will be ideal."

"But Franz," I protested. "I'm hardly dressed for the part."

He brushed my objections aide.

"You can be a Namibian lawyer," he decided. "They are all mad there and nobody wears proper clothing."

To make me look even more like a 'Namibian lawyer,' he produced an expensive looking turquoise sweatshirt, which I wore with my shorts, even though he was dressed to the nines in sports jacket, flannels and tie. The meeting went off without incident and my solemnly frowning 'legal' presence evoked no particular reaction, so perhaps there was method in his apparent insanity.

My days with Franz gave me a rare insight into Gaborone society and some hope for the future of Africa. This was a city where everybody appeared to get along regardless of colour, creed or social status. There was no polarising of communities and all races mingled in absolute freedom. For all its drab interior and water-less countryside, Botswana has enormous mineral wealth. Almost everyone appeared prosperous and was obviously happy in being so, with the result that there were few of the internal conflicts that hampered cultural progress in so many of the countries I pedalled through.

At one stage Franz offered me a job as a sort of trav-elling secretary for one of his numerous companies and I was sorely tempted.

"You would be based in Gaborone," he told me enthusiastically, "but you will travel throughout the sub continent. I need work done in Namibia, South Africa, Zimbabwe and Malawi. As you can see, I don't really approve of hard work myself, so would not expect too much of you."

Fortunately perhaps, he gave me plenty of time to think it over and in the meantime, our relationship took a sudden turn for the worse. It happened over a midday beer on the terrace overlooking the main square and I will never be entirely sure what sparked it off. I think I offered some minor criticism of one of his schemes and he rounded on me, accusing me of being 'just like all the rest.' I protested very mildly, but was then subjected to an objectionable tirade conducted in a heated mixture of English and German with a few smatterings of Tswana thrown in. His emotion suddenly spent, Franz subsided into a sulk and nothing I said or did would pull him out of it. I ordered more beer but he refused to drink it and after forty minutes of this petulance, I rose to my feet and told him I was on my way.

"When you have found what you are looking for, come back and see me," were his parting words and as

I cycled out of Gaborone, I reflected upon them and the man who had uttered them.

That I was searching for something was patently obvious, even to myself but I had no idea what it was. Nor could I figure out what I had done or said to Franz to upset him so. It pained me to leave him the way I did but it seemed – and still does – that it had to be for the best.

A fascinating and captivating man was 'Franz from Austria' but I don't think we would have hit it off in the long run. Perhaps we were too similar in outlook and our ideas on life. On the other hand, I am often accused of being 'laid-back' so perhaps that didn't quite fit in with Franz' mercurial temperament. Like the man itself, it posed quite a conundrum.

I do know that even now, whenever I glance at the turquoise sweat shirt he presented to me after one particularly strange business meeting, I smile inwardly and remember two and a half days spent with an outrageously eccentric adventurer in what must surely have been the happiest and most easy going city, I passed through on my travels.

Mind you, I would love to have seen the Kalahari.

CHAPTER TWELVE

(The Beginning of The End.)

In spite of the fine modern roads and abundant facilities on offer, South Africa seemed a complete anti climax to my venture. As I crossed into the country through the tiny border post at Tlokweng Gate, I had the feeling that the fun was over. There would undoubtedly be hardships and difficulties to come. I would surely meet many more interesting people and I still had a daunting two thousand kilometres ahead of me. But this was now civilised Africa. The challenge had gone. No longer would I face the prospect of excitement and the unknown around every corner. If I was in trouble, help would always be close at hand. If I had problems with the bike, cycle shops were everywhere and they knew all about ATBs.

Suddenly I found myself looking back with considerable nostalgia on the vast expanses of Africa that lay behind me. I remembered with surely unjustified affection the endless, unchanging roads of Zambia and Botswana, the dusty markets where I could haggle with storekeepers and exchange banter with gaily-attired tribesmen and their lady folk. I remembered nights spent in smoky mud huts, packed earth beneath my mattress and lizards eyeing me from flimsy rafters. I thought back to evenings spent around a fire, sparks leaping into the darkness while my host or hostess stirred mealie meal (pap in South Africa) in a blackened iron pot. I remembered the cheerful beer drinks where I lounged among locals, sipping gingerly at sour native brew and tried to follow the ever-louder conversations of those around me. I wouldn't be able to do that again because despite the changes in South African culture over recent years, that sort of mixing is still not encouraged by any of the communities in the Rainbow Nation. Worst of all, I would no longer hear the sobbing cough of lions in the night or sit up for hours in defence of Harriet's virtue against lusting hyenas. I had arrived in civilisation and felt none the better for it. In South Africa, my sleep would be punctuated by the buzz of passing traffic rather than the basic sounds of Nature in the raw. I would not even know another night of deep silence. There would only be the noises of cities, towns and the ubiquitous freeways of modern Africa. The adventurous part of my cycle trip was definitely over and I was suddenly anxious to reach Cape Town.

So it was that I passed through the formalities at Tlokweng Gate with very mixed feelings. My disappointment at adventures end was tinged with a half-suppressed feeling of triumph that I had completed the most difficult part of my venture. From now on, it was merely a question of stamina and if the adventure wasn't there any more – well I had probably had more than enough excitement in any case.

South Africa is a vast land, made up of mountains, plains, harsh, densely-packed forest and coastal regions. The only type of countryside I did not experience on my meandering journey through the Republic was the great, barren desert of the Karoo and I can't say I was sorry about that. I had had more than enough of flat desolation in Botswana. In South Africa, I passed through an incredible variety of scenery, ranging from the austere plains of the Transvaal to the breathtaking ramparts of the Cape and Transkei. I explored coastal fringes and great pine forests and I covered an incredible number of kilometres. In fact, my erratic route through South Africa took in almost as great a distance as had my journey through all five other countries put together.

But any adventure needs an element of risk to make it worthwhile and that was sadly lacking on this last lap. I had been warned *ad infinitum* about the crime rate and security dangers in the country but to me, these risks never seemed quite real. I had heard it all before and still left my bike unlocked without feeling the slightest anxiety about some of the tough-looking characters I met along the way. A lone cyclist – particularly a white one – is an object of curiosity in Africa and is as safe as it is possible to be in the circumstances. My only real danger came from other road users.

Traffic on these broad, fast highways was horrendous. The sheer volume of vehicles was terrifying, particularly as they all seemed to travel at breakneck speed, even allowing for the fact that everything seems fast from a bicycle. On two further occasions I was blown right off my bike and soon decided that riding on the tarmac was just too traumatic, no matter how well maintained that tarmac happened to be. Wherever possible, I used the wide gravel shoulders of the road, although this was often akin to riding on the bumpy bush tracks of Tanzania or Zambia. Once or twice I found myself accidentally riding on a freeway – the three and four lane motorways of South Africa. Not only was that illegal, but it was also distinctly unpleasant, particularly as I needed to keep a wary eye out for traffic policemen as well as homicidal motorists. Those freeway forays were never intentional, but they were hard on the nerves and I was always glad to duck off at the first opportunity, even if it meant going well out of my way.

Another unforeseen problem was fences. To camp comfortably at night, I needed to get well off the road, but in South Africa all open land was surrounded by barbed wire and most gates were securely padlocked. I could understand the reasoning behind this state of affairs, but manhandling a heavily laden bicycle over a two-metre gate was a mammoth undertaking and I spent many a long evening cycling further that I had intended in my efforts to find an unlocked gate or a gap in the barbed wire.

To many people in the world, South Africa is the African success story of the twentieth century. The horrors of *apartheid* have given way to the joys of the Rainbow Nation and despite some very obvious flaws in this comfortable and comforting concept, nobody has ever wanted to believe that the new South Africa cannot succeed.

But there are huge cracks developing in the rosy façade. As in the rest of Africa, official corruption is becoming endemic and the land reclamation programme makes that in Zimbabwe seem tame by comparison. Nearly two thousand white farmers and members of their families have been butchered horribly in their homes and although this is officially put down to criminal activity, it seems far more likely that it is part of the ever-increasing clamour in Africa to give the land back to indigenous people. In general, South Africans are struggling to cement the cracks in society caused by the *apartheid* years and build a worthwhile future for themselves. Tourism is flourishing and if the crime rate is horrendous, the majority of people accept it as the price they have to pay for living in such a beautiful part of the world.

But to understand the problems of any country – and then only to a limited extent – it is necessary to see that country from the viewpoint of local people, particularly those struggling to eke out a living in rural areas. This was something I had tried to do throughout my journey but in the Republic it was far more difficult than it had been anywhere else.

My own impression of South Africans was that they were terribly confused, even after a few years of Independence. The older generation of blacks and whites had been brought up to believe that they were different and they were still struggling to reconcile their ingrained prejudices with what the politically correct world told them was right and proper. It is a process that can and probably will work in the long term, but the process has to take time and is being pushed along too fast by an impatient world. Since their Independence, South Africans had been wrestled into a considerable polarisation of races that will inevitably be difficult to overcome and is terribly destructive in its insularity.

When they are abroad, South Africans are all fiercely nationalistic. At home, they rapidly fall into tribal groupings. Few folk I met proudly proclaimed themselves South African, most preferring to be known as Zulu, Afrikaner, Xhosa or English speaker. Each group tended to look down upon the others and many jokes were doing the rounds that denigrated respective racial groupings. Their development as South Africans had not gone far enough to enable them to laugh collectively and offence was often caused where no offence was intended. With my sister Susan, I attended a play in Johannesburg that poked fun at all the races and it was heartening to see that most of the audience were in fits of laughter. Once the people learn to laugh at themselves, the country will get back on to its feet and prosper. Until then, there are troubles lying in wait and outsiders must refrain from interfering.

It all seemed particularly sad to me, as South Africans must surely rank among the most pleasant and hospitable people in the world. I was welcomed almost everywhere I went, but this was the first country I passed through where I encountered actual hostility as well as kindness and hospitality.

Near Magaliesburg, I was riding gently through a balmy evening when an open lorry, packed full of black schoolchildren moved slowly past. I waved automatically but their gestures were anything but friendly. Their shouted insults and the unabashed hostility on their faces shocked me and left me wondering whether there really was any hope for this wonderful country.

On the other hand, I was cycling through what used to be the Transvaal (Gauteng is so much more difficult to say) one hot afternoon and feeling horribly uncomfortable. Zeerust was behind me, storm clouds were building on the horizon and sweat streamed down my face and body. I was merely going through the motions and progress was desperately slow. I felt decidedly unhappy and as I pedalled, I grew ever more uncomfortable and discontented with my lot. I cursed the heat. I cursed the world and I cursed myself for inflicting such torture on my body. When a big blue car stopped on the verge directly in my path, I cursed it too. I would have to go out on to the tarmac to pass the vehicle and that meant the risk of being flattened by some hurtling behemoth. As if to emphasise these gloomy thoughts, a passing lorry buffeted me so badly that I wobbled precariously before adding that driver too to my list of those worth cursing.

Ten metres behind the stationary car, I glanced back and the road – for once - was clear. As I moved out to pass, I was made to feel thoroughly ashamed of my uncharitable musings when an arm appeared from the driver's window and thrust itself into my path. In the hand on the end of the arm was an open, frosted bottle of beer. I juddered to a stop and stood a little uncertainly astride my bike.

"You look as though you need it," opined the owner of the arm and I couldn't argue with that.

A little hesitantly, I took the beer but once that bottle arrived in the general area of my mouth there was nothing hesitant about my actions. The beer was so cool: so refreshing: so delightfully bitter. It went down without touching the sides. I don't think I paused for breath until the bottle was empty and even then, I shook it to make sure. With a deep sigh of absolute satisfaction, I turned toward the Samaritan. He smiled tightly beneath a grey, toothbrush moustache and thrust another bottle towards me, this time with its cap in place.

"For later on," he told me and while I was juggling with the glassware, he stuck out his hand in introduction.

"Vorster's the name," he told me gruffly and before I could respond with my own, he was off, his engine racing and gravel spurting from beneath his wheels. I was left on the side of the road, uncomfortably draped across my bicycle with one full and one empty bottle in my hands. As the blue car disappeared into the distance, I felt myself somewhat humbled by Mr Vorster's incredible kindness to a complete stranger. I rode on in better mood but shaking my head in perplexity at the infinite humanity of Mankind. Sometimes, it doesn't make sense.

My first major stop in South Africa was to be with my sister in Rivonia, a little way out of Johannesburg. It took me four days to work my way there from the Botswana border and although I didn't meet many people in this massive farming area, there were one or two encounters that made life interesting and kept my spirits from flagging too much.

I remember one gentleman who introduced himself as Mr. B.G Du Preez and I never did find out what the initials stood for. He was an agricultural consultant from Groot Mariko and I met him in Rustenberg. We got to talking and he rescued me from a long wait in the queue for a public telephone by allowing me to contact Suzy Lee from his flat. He told me a great deal about the geology of the area – it being an obvious passion – and made the little lecture even more interesting by accompanying it with a dish of cold mutton and farm cheese. When I hit the road again, he pressed a packet of home made *biltong* on me as well as a bag of fruit that kept me going for days.

Then there was the night I spent in Westonaria at the home of Carmelo Barbaglione, an excitable little Italian builder who was convinced that I was stark staring mad – and made no bones about telling me so. He could not imagine why anyone should wish to travel by bike or – even more horrifying – sleep in the open air. Carmelo was married to a delightfully placid Afrikaans lady and although I was initially taken aback by this unlikely combination of nationalities, he and Marie looked after me really well. For the first time in my life, I even tasted genuine, homemade pasta. What a treat that was.

Terrified by the prospect of losing myself in Johannesburg, I had arranged to rendezvous with Suzy Lee at Roodepoort Hypermarket. As I rode in to that immense complex one Saturday morning, I was tempted to turn around and brave the horrifying traffic to find their house on my own. The entire hypermarket area was a seething mass of hurrying humanity. For one who had grown accustomed to being alone, it was a considerable and very unwelcome culture shock. As usual, I was somewhat dishevelled and as I looked frantically around for help, I spotted a well-dressed dowager surging purposefully toward the hypermarket entrance.

"Excuse me Ma'am," I tentatively addressed the matron, tipping my hat brim in salute and clasping Harriet firmly by the crossbar.

"No!" She barked the word in stentorian tones, sweeping past and leaving me open-mouthed in her wake. In the next few minutes, I had my hand shaken by an earnest young man wanting to try a similar trip for himself and was offered the purchase of a book on dianetics – whatever they might be - for twenty rand, which fortunately I didn't have. Bewildered and battered both mentally and physically, I finally managed to meet up with my family, but my abrupt dismissal by the well-dressed lady rankled and it was not until much later that I was able to see the funny side of it. In my scruffy state she could not possibly have taken me for a salesman, but I suppose I could have been a 'down-and-out' seeking pennies for my next bottle of meths.

It was certainly an abrupt introduction to big city life and left me wondering what I was getting into.

All Johannesburg folk were not like that terrifying dowager however and although the frenetic pace of the city was hard on the nerves, I enjoyed my few days with Sister Susan, her husband John and the other lovely Hammills at their home, beautiful Lusikisiki -Where the Wind Blows. Once again, I was able to eat well, sleep in a bed and relax among people I knew and loved. Despite being in one of the largest and most tumultuous cities in the world, the break undoubtedly did me the world of good.

On my first day back on the road, this was emphasised by the fact that I covered one hundred and fifty four kilometres in nine hours. I cycled continuously with only two short coca cola breaks and from the point of view of distance covered, it was my most successful day of the entire journey by a long way. I couldn't help wondering whether such splendid progress was due to the rest, my desire to get away from Johannesburg or the dish of *waterblommetjies* – pronounced 'vaterblommickys' that Suzy Lee had provided for my supper the previous evening. These are water lily buds and absolutely delicious in a mutton stew. After that enormous one-day effort, I resolved to get some more but never did have the opportunity.

The day ended badly however. I hit my first heavy rain on the approaches to Standerton and the downpour grew more uncomfortable by the moment. I had a yellow rain cape in a pannier and the sudden advent of the deluge necessitated a frantic search for this hitherto unused item of equipment. Inevitably it was beneath my the rest of my kit and by the time I had it ready for wearing, I was drenched. The cape when unfolded looked for all the world like a large yellow toffee paper and as rain lashed my face, I struggled to line my limbs up with corresponding apertures. Eventually, I sorted it all out, remounted Harriet and flapped my soggy way through town like a large yellow refugee from Rowntrees.

Unfortunately, the rain, a howling gale and my arrival, all coincided with the evening rush hour, and I weaved, flapped and wobbled my way through lines of traffic while bemused commuters followed my progress with incredulous expressions. Heavy rods of rain smashed down on the road around me and an added obstacle to progress was the fact that my spectacles just couldn't cope with the volume of water cascading down their panes. I needed windscreen wipers if I was to have any chance of actually seeing where I was going. The cord that held the glasses in position on my face had worn through a couple of days previously, so I could not even take them off without stopping in that horrendous traffic. I was reduced to peering short-sightedly over the top of the sodden specs and hoping that I was heading in the right direction.

It was almost dark when I found my way back on to the open road and the rain showed no sign of abating. I knew that I ought to have stopped off in Standerton, but I had been too busy trying to navigate through the rain. I have always tried not to backtrack in the course of my travels so I just had to keep going.

Cycling slowly through the wet evening, I searched frantically for a suitable camping site, but this was farming country and stout fences barred my passage off the road. Hurtling traffic made riding through the gloom ever more perilous and a sudden puncture put an effective end to forward progress. Fortunately there was a small house a little way off the road and I made for it, guided by the dim glow of a hurricane lamp.

"*Hodi;* is there anybody home?" I called through the driving rain. After a long wait, a middle aged white man emerged through the front door and looked me carefully up and down before offering wary greeting. I don't suppose I was at my most prepossessing.

"I have a puncture and I am very wet," I explained unnecessarily. The wind tore angrily at my toffee paper and I struggled to hold the garment in place. "Would you mind if I slept on your veranda or in one of your sheds?"

There were a number of ramshackle outhouses around the main building and although none of them appeared particularly comfortable, they would at least keep me dry. I had my sights set on the veranda however and waited for his permission to get in out of the rain.

"No," he said abruptly without offering an explanation. "You can sleep in the trees back there."

'Back there' was a small gum plantation, vaguely discernible through the rain and separated from where we stood by a barbed wire fence. I turned away, somewhat shocked by the man's rejection. Hospitality toward strangers is the accepted norm throughout Africa and this was the first time on my trip that I had actually asked for help. I had been turned down flat and felt both angry and disappointed as I walked disconsolately into the wet and windy night. I would not have slept in the man's gum plantation if he had paid me for the pleasure and eventually managed to bed down beneath a spindly tree, closer to the road than the farm buildings.

That was an uncomfortable night but I was to endure many more of those before the trip was over. In the

morning I wasted no time in repairing the puncture
(I was an expert now) and getting away from that unfriendly spot as soon as there was sufficient light to see
what I was doing.

Fortunately the sun was out early, I was able to repack
the toffee paper and I made more excellent progress. The
storm had been an isolated one but it had shown up one
aspect of the world that I had forgotten in my enjoyment
of the simple, hospitable folk I had been living among.

It took me a very long time to regain my good humour.

CHAPTER THIRTEEN

(The Green Hills
of Kwazulu Natal.)

I have always thought of Durban as being like Blackpool with sunshine and hardly my cup of tea. However, my mother was living in Cowies Hill, some twenty kilometres outside the city so I slogged my way across Kwazulu Natal to see her.

In Tanzania, the hills had been cruel but they were interspersed with wide plains where weary muscles could rest and my battered spirit had a chance to recover. In Kwazulu Natal there were just hills, hills and more hills. Shortly after crossing into the province at Volksrust, I found myself up in the clouds and from there it was up and down all the way to Pietermaritzburg – nearly five hundred kilometres of fairly hellish cycling.

There were surprisingly few people on the road in this section so I had little chance to talk. When I did get into conversation, I was too weary to say much but perhaps this was as well. Those locals I did see gazed at me with the same apathetic acceptance I had encountered in Zimbabwe, while passing motorists made me feel like an exotic goldfish by the way that they stared. I was often tempted to stick my tongue out but held myself in check. After all, I was a guest in their country so I suppose they had a right to be curious. It was terribly off-putting though and made me cross.

In Johannesburg, I had bought new inner tubes for Harriet, feeling that for the little benefit they provided, the solid tubes were causing too much damage to the tyres themselves. They also made pedalling a great deal more difficult. Now I was back in civilisation, I felt that I could cope with punctures but it was a decision I was to regret and never more so that when I was toiling through Kwazulu Natal. Just north of Newcastle, I suffered three punctures in quick succession and took advantage of a local caravan and camping site to give all four inner tubes a thorough check over. I applied patches to every spot that even looked as though it might give way but it was all for nothing. I suffered my forty-fifth puncture within half an hour of starting out the next morning.

That Newcastle stopover did save me from sleeping out in a most amazing thunderstorm however. Purple clouds had been building up throughout the evening and the pyrotechnics began shortly after I had retired to my sleeping bag. Lightning crackled and ripped across the sky, while thunder seemed to shake the ground on which I lay. The air smelled wet and smoky while the heavy atmosphere made breathing difficult. There was a thatched sun shelter in one corner of the caravan park so I pulled Harriet and my bedding into its doubtful protection, from where we watched the storm. It was certainly spectacular. Water smashed, steamed and sizzled on the ground around us and the air turned cold and decidedly clammy. Huddling in my bag, I marvelled at the furious power of Nature. It was truly awe-inspiring and

I thanked my lucky stars – and the *tokoloshe* of course –
that I had not been sleeping out in the open

After one particularly hot morning, in the course of
which I had climbed two enormous hills as well as a
number of gentler ones, I passed through the five thou-
sandth kilometre of my trip. It seemed cause for celebra-
tion, so I marked the achievement in the grand manner
with an ice cream at Mooi Rivier. I would have preferred
something a little stronger, but it was Sunday and in
Afrikanerdom, no alcohol is served on the Lord's Day.
Nevertheless I was very pleased with myself and moved
on feeling good.

After Mooi Rivier I found myself climbing again but
towards evening, the road dropped away and I enjoyed
a headlong downhill dash for the next twenty-six kilometres. It was exhilarating to hurtle through the bends
and watch tiny hamlets flashing by. The area must have
originally been settled by Scottish pioneers and I smiled
as signboards reminiscent of the Highlands flashed by.
This was cycling with a difference. It certainly wasn't the
slogging drudgery I had become accustomed to over the
weeks. Arriving at Howick and the Midmar Dam just as
darkness was falling, I was breathless with the excitement of it all.

I had breakfast in Pietermartizburg the following
morning and enjoyed watching the commuters from the
vantage of my pavement table. Mountains of egg, bacon
and crispy sausages taste doubly delicious when one has
time to relax and enjoy the curious stares of envious
people hurrying off to work. Feeling replete and content,
I pedalled slowly out of this picturesque little frontier

town, then it was downhill all the way – nearly – to Cowies Hill and Mama. I was hot, tired and sweaty when I knocked at the door of 9 Chandler Road to be greeted by my mother in curlers. This grand old lady has never quite grown accustomed to the eccentricities of her only son and hadn't had any idea when I would be arriving, but she carried off the meeting with aplomb.

"You look around one hundred and ten," she commented mildly and I wasn't sure whether she meant in age or temperature. I didn't follow it up for fear of further damage to my morale and there followed a pleasant few days in the bosom of my family. I visited my other sisters in Durban North and Gillots and almost – only 'almost' you'll notice - grew tired of recounting my adventures along the road. Wide-eyed nephews listened agog as I spoke and my brothers in law treated me with all the wary respect due to any wandering lunatic, but it was all great fun.

<hr />

There is one part of Durban that has always fascinated me and that is the Indian Market. I had spent many happy hours there in the past but on this occasion I was saddened to see that modern bureaucracy had struck even there. Atmosphere had been sacrificed to the cause of public health and that wonderful shambles of a meeting place didn't seem the same. In the past, stalls had been piled haphazardly together, the smell of spices blending cheerfully with the gentle aroma of sandalwood and the pungent scent of fresh – and not so fresh – fish. Shrill voices importuned the milling customers and gabbled vastly exaggerated descriptions of exotic merchandise. The languages used originated from lands as far apart as Bengal, Belfast and the Cape Flats but everyone seemed to understand. The whole place was a seething, surging mass of excited humanity and even for a loner like me, it was a fascinating place to visit.

The market had changed. It had become far more hygienic and stallholders were required by law to keep their shops clean. The drama of the place had disappeared, even though the wares on offer were the same – carvings in wood, ivory (few countries in Southern Africa seemed to abide by the CITES convention on ivory trading) and Birmingham plastic; garments ranging from silk saris to boxer shorts and spicy foods in abundance. The stallholders made as much noise as ever and I was offered everything from a camphor chest at 'special price only to you, Sir' to a ticket in the Zimbabwe National Lottery. Quite how that particular item got there I shall never know.

Yet there was something missing. Printed receipts were being issued to customers and the frenetic excitement of the old market had been replaced by a more modern order of business. I almost expected to see people queuing for service and would not be surprised if that is the case when next I visit. I left the market building reflecting that without the shrill haggling and totally unhygienic atmosphere of the past, the Indian Market of Durban was a great disappointment. Truly, progress in Africa has a great deal to answer for. This great, unregulated continent is rapidly succumbing to the empty blandishments of hygienists, sociologists and other zealots who seem intent on making it as sterile and unromantic as their own uninteresting lands.

I did have one horrible experience in Durban that will live on in my mind for a very long time. I was cycling quietly past Kingsmead Gardens and stopped at traffic lights on a wide section of road. A cheerful Indian pedestrian carrying a brightly flowered umbrella crossed in front of me and waved a friendly greeting. A few metres on, he was hit by a car, racing up behind and unable to stop in time.

The impact made an awful sound and the poor bloke was hurled high in the air. He was very dead when I checked on him and there was nothing I could do but as I rode on, my heart bled for the fellow and I shall have an abiding Durban memory of bloody daisies and savagely twisted umbrella spokes lying accusingly in the road.

Even the Durban sea front had changed for the worse since my previous visit. The modernisers had stepped in and the long, hectic stretch of shoreline I remembered had been concreted over and tidied up so that the resemblance to Blackpool, Bournemouth – or even Battersea – was even more pronounced. The rolling breakers were as fearsome as ever, but I couldn't help wishing that the modern planners had left it alone. Even the fearsome rickshaw drivers who had so intimidated me in my youth turned out to be little old men, dressed in faded clothing beneath their exotic finery. It was all rather disappointing.

<hr />

Suddenly I was fretting to finish my journey. I still had seventeen hundred kilometres ahead of me, but I was bored now and fed up with the traumas of travel. Each day was no longer a separate adventure and the hills all looked the same. I wanted to rest, to have a change from aching muscles, a sore backside and the endless boredom of unchanging road. I wanted a change from roadside people too. I needed conversation with friends and loved ones, not the stilted chat of strangers meeting for the first time.

But there was still a long way to go and I toiled down the Natal South Coast, moving from resort to resort and meeting the blank, sun-struck stares of holiday-makers with as much aplomb as I could muster. I gorged myself on fast foods and ice cream but I was always anxious to move on. This was all too civilised, too sterile and too much like holiday Europe rather than Africa. It was with a feeling of relief that I turned inland from Port Alfred and entered the rolling hill country of the Transkei.

I had been warned about this little province through-out the South African section of my journey. It might have been Nelson Mandela's homeland but South Africans – including my own family – seemed to share a certain paranoia about the place.

"Be very careful in the Transkei," they would mutter warningly. "The crime rate is appalling and you will have to watch out for your life as well as your possessions. Don't sleep out and be careful not to speak with strangers."

That was a laugh. I had been speaking to strangers for months and it was one of the reasons for undertaking the venture in the first place. As for sleeping out, slumber beneath the stars was one of the major joys of the entire trip.

But the warnings were given with my best interests at heart and as I toiled through the first of many Transkei mountain passes, I wondered why South Africans should be quite so paranoid about this particular part of their country. It was one of the original *apartheid* 'black homelands' and sociologists would probably claim that their fears were racist in origin, but to me that was the convenient answer and far too simplistic.

All of us are wary about places we know nothing about. In Kenya I was warned against the Tanzanians. They in turn claimed that local banditry all emanated from Zambia and the Zambians looked on my own compatriots as brigands and thugs. I have mentioned elsewhere in this narrative that one needs to descend to grass roots level to even begin to understand a country and its people. South Africans invariably speed through Transkei on their way to somewhere else, pausing only briefly in the larger towns and usually in a hurry to reach their ultimate destination. They don't speak with the locals so have no idea how those locals live or think. This leads to mutual distrust and the widely held belief on the part of most South Africans that the people of Transkei are all criminals.

There probably is a great deal of crime in this beautiful little corner of South Africa, yet I saw no evidence of undue dishonesty in the Transkei. I could only take the people as I found them and that was as being among the most cheerful and hospitable communities in Southern Africa. I made no attempt to alter my mode of travel for the sake of security and felt as safe in the Transkei as I did anywhere else.

In fact it was a marvellous country to cycle through with some of the most breathtaking scenery in Africa. I was battered by fierce crosswinds during my first couple of days but the magnificence of my surroundings helped alleviate the discomfort of pedalling. Majestic ranges, forested gorges and occasional glimpses of the distant sea; rustic villages nestling against sweeping hillsides and the inevitable piles of wrecked and rusted machinery that are littered around the continent, could be seen on all sides. I passed football fields where grazing livestock kept the grass down and small black pigs ignored me as they joggled across the road. One morning my progress was slowed by fog and I spent a couple of hours moving gingerly along the side of a mountain road, wondering what lay ahead. The lack of visibility did nothing to slow the pace of other road users and I eventually found myself a reasonably comfortable spot on a wet hillside and sat it out in my toffee paper cape.

Local hospitality was typically African. At the first trading post I came to, the lady proprietor was sitting in her dressing gown and pyjamas – it was early afternoon – getting her accounts up to date and when she learned that I was going all the way to Cape Town, she pressed cool drink and cake upon me, while begging me to send her a post card when I reached my destination. I did too and hope she enjoyed it.

I couldn't get over the fact that everyone in this part of the world seemed to look on the Cape as being incredibly distant, even though I felt I was almost there. The major part of my journey was behind me and the few hundred kilometres that remained didn't worry me at all.

A chance roadside meeting resulted in my staying with Peter and Lynn Barnes in their Umtata home and like so many others along the way, they did their best to ensure that I was properly fed, washed and rested before allowing me to continue southward. Lynn was born in the same month as me, so I suppose it was inevitable that we should get on, while her parents, Johnny and Hantie Theron really did me proud. They worked at a mission school for the disabled at Effata which means 'the blind can see and the deaf can hear' outside Umtata and Johnny obviously enjoyed showing me around his woodwork class for deaf youngsters. The school was run by the Dutch Reformed Church and I couldn't help reflecting that those devout and kindly Afrikaners did so much for black people in their care, despite being regarded as out and out racists in much of the world. Africa is a cruel land for those who do not have all their faculties and although nobody actually shuns the disabled, there are few amenities laid on to make their lives any easier. At Effata, every effort was made to create ideal conditions for the students and fit them for life in the outside world. History has given the Afrikaners a bad reputation, but at Effata, a gentler side to this fiercely proud nation was on view to anyone who cared to take a look.

Johnny took me down to Koffee Bay one afternoon and I felt truly humbled as I gazed out from the cliffs toward the 'hole in the wall.' This is a vast tunnel carved by wave action in a great black rock and I marvelled at the awesome power of that maelstrom of heaving white water, where the Indian Ocean thrashed itself into foamy frustration against the cliffs. Not for nothing was this known as 'The Wild Coast' and many a great ship had already dashed itself to pieces against those fearsome cliffs. I felt sure that no matter what protective measures were put in force, there would be many more wrecks to come.

Two days after leaving the Barnes family, I met Anyosisye Nyasalandi outside another trading store. He was a former civil servant eking out a precarious living as a subsistence farmer near Umtata. We had lunch at his home and he seemed unduly pessimistic about the future of the new South Africa.

"It is all very well calling this the Rainbow Nation," he muttered darkly, "but the colours of any rainbow are all separate. Mandela is from here himself, but already he wants us to forgo our Independence and become part of South Africa. We have been on our own since 1976 and are quite capable of looking after our own economy, yet he wants to swallow us up."

Almost absently, he rolled a handful of mealie meal (*mpufu* in the Transkei) into a ball and dipped it into a bowl of gravy before continuing.

"We don't want to be part of South Africa. We supported the ANC in its struggle but we have our own government and want to be ruled by our own elected politicians. They may not be clever men, but they are ours and know how this country works. What do those people in Johannesburg and Pretoria know about the Transkei?"

He had a point too, although I was not as sanguine about the economic capabilities of the Transkei government as he was. In Koffee Bay, I had seen two large hotels standing derelict, even though they were magnificent buildings in superb positions overlooking the ocean. They had been built by the former national leader, Kaisa Matanzima while he had been in power, but local gossip had it that he ran them entirely for the benefit of his friends and cronies. When he was ousted in a coup, his successors sacked all the staff and allowed the hotels to run down into ruin. As is the way with coups in Africa, everything pertaining to the previous regime was abandoned and forgotten.

I had a personal interest in that little piece of African history. My very first novel, Ivory Madness had been on the prescribed list of books for Transkei schools when the coup took place and had sadly taken its place among other mementoes of the former regime, to be thrown out by the new government. However that had little to do with the current state of the economy and although I told Anyosisye the story, I soon forgot it in my interest at what he was saying.

"They have built a new government headquarters in Umtata," he went on. "It is a wonderful building but it remains empty because the government have spent all their budgeted money and cannot afford to buy the necessary furniture. The building even has its own helicopter pad, which cost millions of rands, but it will remain unused for a very long time. I'll guarantee that the South Africans won't help us with that. They will be too busy worrying about their own slum dwellers in Soweto and places like that."

I saw the edifice in question while I was in Umtata and the sight of an old man urinating against the side of the empty building seemed to tell its own story.

Yet, like their counterparts in Kenya, Tanzania, Zambia and Botswana, the people of Transkei proved to be cheerful, kindly folk and I was hailed by almost everyone I passed on that winding road through the mountains. Water or a cool drink were given freely and the smiles cast in my direction were always friendly. I had no fears for Harriet's safety and felt no worries about leaving her unattended and unsecured beside the road.

It is a spectacular corner of Southern Africa, the Transkei and I only hope that when the Rainbow Nation finally sorts out its teething problems, this little nation will be left alone to make its own decisions – even if they are the wrong ones.

The Barnes family were lovely folk and were extremely interested in my adventures along the road. When I left, they suggested that I call in at the little farm they ran near East London, I was only too pleased to agree. The farm nestles among the border hills and Peter and Lynn built the homestead themselves, motoring down from Umtata over a period of years before it took shape.

"It was backbreaking work," Lynn told me enthusiastically, "but it was worth it in the end."

With that I could only agree. The picturesque homestead sat on the crest of a hill and the views were truly fantastic. Green hillsides, deep, wooded ravines and on the horizon, the distant blue of the Indian Ocean. Angora goats peered curiously at me from a nearby pen and in the distance I could see four ostrich strutting arrogantly along a fence line. At daybreak I went for a long walk and once again felt that I had discovered a spot where a person could find real peace. A deep silence hung over the crystal cold of the *veldt* and it was broken only by the distant call of a *picannin* and the whistle of a yellow-billed kite circling high above my head. There were no traffic noises, no clatter of machinery and no industrial smog to mar the clarity of the atmosphere. I felt truly alone and alive.

But idyllic though it was, I had a date to keep in Cape Town and was anxious to be back on the road. Regretfully, I bade Lynn and Peter a fond farewell and rode on south once more.

I hope one day to return to the Transkei and if I have to use a bicycle again to appreciate it, then that is the way I will travel.

CHAPTER FOURTEEN

(The Wet and Windy Cape)

At the end of our 1963 trip, we had arrived in Cape Town late in the evening. Dusty, tired and travel-stained, we asked a passer by for a nearby hotel and ended up at the Mount Nelson – one of the most luxurious establishments in Africa and an experience in itself. Bed and breakfast had set us back five rand fifty apiece – an enormous sum of money in those days. We hadn't been able to afford dinner as well, so had sneaked into town for a sandwich. The following day we moved to a less expensive hostelry but our night at 'The Nellie' had been a high spot for all of us and inspired much amused conversation over succeeding years.

While cycling through Zambia I had written to my agent, Frances Bond in Durban and suggested that the management of the Mount Nelson might like to round off my cycling venture in the grand manner, by putting me up for my last night on the road. With its five star rating, I didn't doubt that a night at The Nellie would cost a great deal more than five rand fifty, but it seemed well worth a try.

When presented with the original receipt, General Manager Nick Seewer was enthusiastic and offered both

Frances and I two nights with full board thrown in. It was more than I could have expected and the prospect of such luxury to come kept me going through many a bleak period when I longed to give it all up and go home. When we met in Durban, Frances promised to arrange press coverage for my arrival in Cape Town and I blithely told her that I would be there for 10 am on Thursday 27[h] October. For the first time since leaving Nairobi, I had given myself a deadline and this led to frequent calculations of distance and time over succeeding weeks. On leaving East London, I reckoned that I needed to cover only eighty kilometres a day to make Cape Town on time.

North of the Zambezi my daily average had been slightly less than this, but that was when the road surfaces were rough and adventure beckoned from every bend in the road. Since crossing that great river, I had managed a daily hundred kilometres without undue effort and this was not only due to the improved road surfaces. When I was bored or not enjoying myself, the only thing to do was cycle hard and forget everything else in the torment of straining muscles.

So eighty kilometres a day over the final fortnight did not seem too daunting a prospect, although the one factor I hadn't taken into account was the weather.

<hr>

The Cape Province is recognised by travellers everywhere as being one of the most beautiful places in the world. Vasco da Gama or one of the other navigating immortals of ages past described it as 'this – the fairest cape of all' and I reckon he had it about right. The Cape has everything going for it. Great rocky ranges, rolling downs, vine-covered hillsides and vast forests of pine and conifer stretch toward vast, curving horizons. Pretty little towns nestle among the hills and a truly magnificent coastline adds to its raw beauty. The 'Garden Route' is the recommended tourist route from Durban to Cape Town and it leads one through the most delightful places.

This was the route I took, both with the Rendles in 1963 and on my travels with Harriet. The road wound down the long coastline, taking in gleaming white villages that hadn't changed in two centuries, great black forests and ravines that drove the breath back into my throat when I peered into their precipitous depths. I felt that I was riding through a little corner of heaven on earth and it should have provided a fitting end to my ride through the magnificence of Africa.

It would have too, had it not been for the weather. The Weather Spirit of the Matopos seemed to have forgotten the money I had given him or else he didn't feel it was enough, because he let me down badly in the Cape.

Throughout that last fortnight, it rained. No, that is not quite correct – it bucketed down. To add to the difficulties, a strong wind blew the rain in stinging stair rods against my face as I struggled along. With my head down against the fury of driving water, I had little opportunity to appreciate the beauty of my surroundings and I grew thoroughly fed up with having wet clothes and squelching with every movement. My sleeping bag developed an overall covering of mould and the punctures continued. There can surely be no more depressing occupation than changing a bicycle wheel in heavy rain, no matter how spectacular the surrounding scenery.

On one particularly wet and windy afternoon I was riding hard from Humansdorp when my rear wheel went down. I took shelter beneath a road bridge formed by an

overcrossing highway and duly replaced the damaged
tube before sitting down with a bubbling pipe to wait
out the storm. I was determined not to go out again until
the rain stopped. Water dripped from the concrete road-
way above my head and throughout a long, cold afternoon, I huddled miserably in my toffee paper, wondering
what I was doing so uncomfortable, cold and far from
home. When the wet world around me began to darken,
I decided that the rain was not going to stop, so I dragged
Harriet and my bedding up into the eaves of the bridge
and settled down for a restless night. The road above my
head was not a busy one but every time a vehicle passed,
the resulting rumble only centimetres from my face
disturbed my slumbers and threatened to send me sliding
down the steep slope on which I lay. I was a memorable
night but for all the wrong reasons.

I used my bivvy frequently on this section of the trip,
but the retaining cords needed to be securely tied against
the fury of that ever-present wind. The weather kept
most people indoors and I seemed to go for days without speaking to anyone other than shopkeepers or wait-
resses. Most of them stared at me in undisguised amazement and some were abrupt to the point of rudeness. I'm
not sure what they thought I was doing but my appearance obviously disconcerted them, even though the
prevalence of well-serviced garages ensured that I remained reasonably tidy.

In one such tearoom, a sweet-faced young coloured
girl recognised my accent and asked me whether I came
from Zimbabwe. She hailed from Bulawayo and we spent
a pleasant forty minutes chatting about the problems
besetting our country. When I cycled on again, I carried
a gift of hot chips and memories of a lovely young exile

to brighten my evening. In normal circumstances, that good lady probably would not have even noticed a middle-aged and decidedly rumpled traveller, but in the shared loneliness of being away from home, we had immediately become friends, despite my appearance.

Just north of Port Elizabeth I tired of my nightly discomfort and went into a campsite, intent on a good nights sleep. The Afrikaans lady in reception peered at me in horror.

"We don't allow motor cyclists in here," she told me sternly and when I pointed out that Harriet hardly deserved such accreditation, she enlarged the ban to include ATB riders as well. I suppose I looked pretty bedraggled but I rode on reflecting that the Cape Afrikaner could learn a great deal about hospitality from his Transvaal counterpart.

This opinion was strengthened in George when I tried to book a chalet in the municipal camping grounds. The couple in the front office were actively discouraging and I moved on feeling decidedly anti social. Rather than allow myself further embarrassment, I resolved to sleep rough from there on. After all, I had the Mount Nelson to look forward to and that prospect would surely sweeten any further unpleasantness I might encounter over the next couple of weeks.

As I drew closer to Cape Town, I became ever more nervous about mixing with people again and the reception that had been laid on for me suddenly seemed an event to be avoided. I dreaded the fanfare involved and suddenly did not want to be with people. I wondered whether I should just turn around and head back to Nairobi. In fact, I felt thoroughly miserable about life in general and the Cape Province in particular.

Yet there were marvellous moments on this last portion of my trip. The scenery was indeed magnificent and I spent hours sitting on ridge or rise and just gazing about me at damp hillsides and distant horizons. Where I could, I slept in pine forests and enjoyed waking to the fragrance of sweet wood and a bedroom ceiling of distant treetops high above my head. In the great Tsitsikamma Forest, I stopped early for the day, worked my way well off the road and set up my bivvy in a particularly deep section of the forest. Here I sat out the afternoon and evening, sitting outside my little shelter like a Cherokee chief, very much at home with my comforting pipe and the serenity of my surroundings.

On another occasion, I felt more like an Australian swagman than a Native American. I rode well into a blustery evening in my search for shelter and eventually camped beside a small pond in windy, sheep-covered plains. A fallen tree provided support for my bivvy and I spent the evening drinking hot tea to keep out the chill.

And of course there was always the sea. At the top of every rise, I would stop and gaze out to my left. That blue patch I could see beneath the haze was the Indian Ocean and there were times when I could almost smell its salty essence. I thought I could at any rate.

Near Knysna, three elderly ladies stopped to lend a hand when Harriet's chain inexplicably leapt off its sprockets and they kindly offered to take my panniers on to the next town so that I could ride unencumbered for a while. It was a tempting offer but I regretfully turned them down.

"You can trust us," one old dear told me sweetly. "We won't run off with your things."

It was hardly a question of trust. There was nothing in my belongings to make them worth pinching but I was reluctant to hand them over, as it would mean that I had to reach a specific destination that day. It was something I had tried to avoid from the start of the trip. Aims and goals seemed all very well, but they put limitations on my wandering journey and I didn't want that. I never aimed at a specific daily mileage and whenever I found a pleasant spot, I was able to stop and enjoy it for as long as I wanted. The ladies seemed to understand my stammering explanations and I rode on, fully kitted out but cheered by their kindly offer of assistance.

I suppose it was inevitable that as Cape Town and journeys-end drew closer, so my nervousness increased in leaps and bounds. With three days to go, I was in a state of pure funk. I was facing a return to the real world and didn't know how I would cope. I would have to grow accustomed to being with people on a permanent basis – no longer able to bid them farewell and set off on my own whenever I felt like it. I would be faced with the daily struggles of life in society and would even have to consider earning my living again. I would have to worry about time too and that was a horrible prospect. No longer would my parameters of existence be merely those of the open road and no longer would I be able to sleep when I felt like it or eat merely because I was hungry. It all seemed horribly daunting and my anticipation of imminent arrival at my destination was tinged with deep disappointment that the venture would soon be over.

Once again, I considered avoiding the official reception. Perhaps I could reach Cape Town, take a few photographs and then cycle back again. I seriously considered that option for a while but – somewhat reluctantly

– abandoned it as being impractical. I was in no state for a return journey. Besides, I had had more then enough of cycling, particularly in such abominable weather. Both Harriet and I were desperately in need of a long rest and the very fact that thoughts of a return journey had crossed my mind made me cycle even harder toward Cape Town and the end of my journey.

Four hundred kilometres to go and I woke up one morning to find that a tin of condensed milk had leaked in a pannier and the box of solid fuel tablets had split. The resultant mess of small sticky squares did little for my early morning equanimity and I was not in a happy frame of mind when I set out once more.

The sun was high in the sky and I was toiling sweatily up a long hill when a big land cruiser skidded to a stop ahead of me. Instinctively I glanced at the registration plate, hesitated then looked again. It was definitely Zambian. Excitement flared in my breast. Surely it couldn't be...? But it was.

Don and Maryanne Burton piled out of the vehicle and came running back towards me. Moments later we were dancing around the tarmac in enthusiastic reunion, much to the consternation of passing motorists.

"What a wonderful surprise," Maryanne bubbled. "We didn't expect to see you again. When Don said it was you, I just couldn't believe it."

"I recognised the hat." Don told us smugly.

The Burtons were on their way to Cape Town for a short break and had almost forgotten the shabby stranger who had spent the weekend at Mufandzalo all those months before. It seemed an incredible coincidence that we should come together again so many thousands of kilometres from Kabwe. They would only be in Cape Town for a few days and when I mentioned my proposed reception on the 17th, they both looked genuinely disappointed.

"We leave on that day," Don muttered. "Perhaps we can make a plan but it might be difficult."

It was a little too much to hope for but that little roadside meeting certainly made my day and when they finally left me, I cycled on in a totally changed frame of mind. I even sang for a little while and startled the local bird life.

A few kilometres further on, I came to a farm store. In the Cape, these establishments serve light meals of delicious variety and I pulled in, hoping for breakfast. The young proprietor was apologetic.

"I'm expecting a party of sixty for breakfast at any minute," He told me with a shrug. "I'll never be able to fit you in."

It didn't matter and I prepared to move on but he had followed me outside and seen the bike.

"Where have you come from?" He asked and when I told him, he took me by the arm.

"Never let it be said that I turned away a man who has cycled that far. Come on in. We'll find somewhere for you."

I ended up tucking into a magnificent breakfast on an upturned orange box, set up in the centre of the shop. The sixty-strong party duly arrived and if they were curious about the bedraggled apparition among the display counters, they refrained from comment. The way that the management catered to my needs at such obvious inconvenience to themselves enhanced what had already been a lovely day and I was whistling when I left to the cheery good wishes of the breakfasters.

⟡

Cape Town – 100 kilometres.

I could scarcely believe the sign. After four and a half months on the road, I was almost there. It was early evening and I had just shared a flask of sweet black coffee with a young Capetonian named Ronnie Claasen who had stopped his car for a chat.

"One more range of hills and you are there," Ronnie told me. "It is easy going from there on and you should make it tomorrow without any difficulty."

But 'tomorrow' was only the 26th and my appointment with the Press was not until the following day. I camped high in the hills that evening and then meandered slowly on, my destination growing ever nearer and depression once more gripping my soul. Looking down on Somerset West and The Strand from Sir James Lowrie's pass, I reflected that Cape Town lay over the next horizon and my journey was virtually over. I sped down the curves of the pass feeling ineffably sad that I would soon have to forsake the free and easy life of a cycling Gypsy.

Apart from Ronnie Claasen, the Cape Afrikaners had left me with a somewhat jaundiced view of their hospitality but I was soon forced to revamp my opinions.

I was walking slowly along the magnificent sea front of The Strand, Harriet trundling beside me and both of us enjoying the beauty of the scene, when I was stopped for a chat by a young man walking his dog. He was interested in my journey and questioned me at length about the spread of AIDS in the continent and the work being done by various Christian fellowships. I could tell him little about the dread disease but regaled him with a couple of anecdotes about the Butlers and other religious folk I had met along the way.

We parted with a handshake and I crossed the road to a novelty shop where a sign proclaimed the availability of ice cream. I had a sudden urge for a treat and handed over the requisite change to a jovial lady behind the counter. Her thick accent betrayed her Afrikaans origins and she chatted cheerfully while we waited for the ice cream machine to produce its precious contents.

The phone rang while we waited and she addressed it in Afrikaans for a while and then returned to hand me back the one rand eighty I had paid for the ice cream. I raised my eyebrows and she tinkled into laughter.

"That was my husband on the phone," she explained. "He says that I should be ashamed to take your money after you have cycled such a long way. What must you be thinking of us?"

I assured her that my thoughts had been nothing if not amiable, but pocketed the money and tucked into my cone – all the more delicious for the kindness what had accompanied it.

While I had my face buried in coloured ice cream, the young man I had spoken to previously entered the shop and greeted me with obvious relief.

"Meneer," he said in his stilted English. "I was thinking when I left you that I would enjoy to buy you breakfast."

It was midday and well past the normal time for such a repast but I was only too pleased to accompany him to a nearby restaurant where we discussed religion and the politics of Africa over steak, egg and chips. I left Harriet in the care of the shop lady who gleefully threatened to charge anyone entering her establishment 'just for looking at your *lekker* little barcycle."

Campher Serfontein was a law student at Stellenbosch University and we enjoyed an excellent meal together. Very religious and a little narrow in his outlook, he questioned me closely on my travels, placing much emphasis on missionaries and the 'turning of the heathen to Christ.' These were not subjects dear to my heart, but the meal was a generous gesture on his part and I enjoyed the time I spent in his company.

When we parted, Campher gave me directions as to the easiest way to enter Cape Town and by mid afternoon, my '*lekker* little barcycle' and I had embarked on the very last lap.

CHAPTER FIFTEEN

(The End of a Dream)

I was almost there and my last journal entry before Cape Town rather sums up the ambivalence of my feelings.

26th October

'*My last night on the road and I am not at all sure how I feel. Harriet lies on the sand in front of me and she looks in a sorry state. Her paintwork is chipped and scratched, the transfers picked up along the way already peeling and only vaguely decipherable. The gear cable has almost frayed right through but it has been like that for the last five hundred odd kilometres and I'm close enough now to push us both in if necessary. As for me, I am thin, sunburned and ragged, but the scars are only skin deep and inside I feel a quiet sense of elation in spite of my nervousness about the morrow. I have made it now in spite of all the warnings received before and during the trip. Cycling from Nairobi to Cape Town is fairly commonplace nowadays and not a feat that merits headlines, but it means a great deal to me. I have proved something to myself – if only that I am not too old for adventure after all.*'

Crossroads and Kyelitsha Townships were notorious places throughout South Africa for three decades or more. Untidy expanses of high-density housing, they were little more than vast slums, but they were home to millions of black and coloured people and according to local folklore were hotbeds of intrigue, drug taking and dastardly deeds.

There are few genuinely black people in the Cape Province of South Africa, most of the indigenous population being of Cape Coloured stock, descended from Malays, Indians and the indigenous races. Those coloured folk I came in contact with were cheerful and friendly, although I had been a little shocked at a hamlet near Mossel Bay to find almost the entire population drunk out of their skulls at eight on a Sunday morning. There must have been a tremendous party going on through the preceding night. Nevertheless they had all been friendly and I spent half an hour repairing punctures at a local garage where the only sober citizen around was the black proprietor.

My last night on the road was spent in a grove of trees between the N2 freeway and one or other of the townships. I was a little nervous about my proximity to so much potential criminality but it was the only place I could find so close to Cape Town and I carefully brushed my tracks from the path before making camp.

Darkness was falling when a band of youths passed along the path and much to my horror, one of them ran into the trees to spend a penny. He was heading directly for me and I watched in awful fascination as he did what he had to do, not ten metres from where I sat on my spread sleeping bag.

As he prepared to rejoin his mates, he stopped abruptly and my heartbeat quickened. Crouching down for a better view, he peered through the undergrowth at Harriet, perched in full view on top of a small rise. Discovery seemed inevitable and I prepared to get to my feet and make my presence known.

For some strange reason, that lad was not too sure what he was seeing. Perhaps it was too dark to make it out properly from where he stood, although to me the bicycle seemed all too obvious. I stayed where I was, totally motionless while he moved this way and that, even raising himself on to his toes in order to get a better view. I suppose a bright yellow – albeit somewhat battered – mountain bike is hardly what one expects to find in the Cape Flats and he couldn't quite believe the evidence of his own eyes.

How long we remained in our respective positions I have no way of knowing but to me, it seemed like half a lifetime. I was a little below the youngster's line of vision and perfectly still so he didn't see me, but when he seemed to make up his mind and rushed off to rejoin his cronies, I felt sure it was only a matter of time before they returned to investigate the unexpected booty.

What then, I asked myself. Would they take Harriet from me – rob me of what little I had left? Would they mug me and leave me for dead in that isolated spot? It all seemed so sad that I should have travelled so far, only to come to grief on my very last night. How I wished I had kept on for Cape Town that afternoon and slept in the city. I was a mere twenty-eight kilometres away and it would have been so easy.

But it was too late for that and I waited anxiously for inevitable discovery and whatever might follow. Inwardly quoting the proverb about bolting horses and stable doors, I moved Harriet to a different position and

camouflaged my sleeping bag before settling down to
wait for I knew not what.

The youths never returned, so whether the lad hadn't
believed the evidence of his own eyes or whether the
others had scoffed at his story, I shall never know.
Perhaps they were merely honest youngsters and I was
being overly paranoid. Whatever the case, I enjoyed a
quiet night, although for the first time in weeks, I was
harried by mosquitoes. As I had given my net to Graeme
when I was out at his camp, there was little I could do
about the horrid little pests.

Feeling a little like a hippy high on pot, I cycled into town
the following morning. I had been directed on to the N2
by a traffic policeman who brushed aside my reserva-
tions as to the legality of using the freeway.

"Ag, nobody worries about that," he assured me
heartily. "All the long distance fellows come in that way."

Nobody else might have worried but I hadn't been half
an hour on the road before I was very worried indeed.
I was caught up in the morning rush hour and the volume
of traffic was truly terrifying. As usual, the commuting
motorists were lost in their own problems and paid scant
attention to the tribulations of an overladen cyclist.
Rather shakily, I realised that I wasn't there yet.

Weaving in and out of vehicles, I negotiated several
hold ups and then found myself deep in the maelstrom
of what had to be the busiest road in the city. There were
five lanes of hurtling traffic and me. My heart pounded
and for the second time in my months on the road, I was
genuinely scared. I could not possibly survive another
ten kilometres of this dangerous chaos, but nor could

I turn back. At one point, I was forced to cross two lanes of filtering traffic to regain the side of the freeway and I stood for nearly fifteen minutes, waiting for a suitable gap. Everyone must have seen my predicament, but not one of those hurrying commuters thought to give me a break and let me through. The wind of passing vehicles buffeted my shoulders and my nervousness increased by the second. I was back in the civilised world with a vengeance.

Eventually I took my waning courage in both hands, murmured a prayer to Whoever was listening and dashed across in front of two hurtling vehicles. Frenzied blaring of horns, shaking of fists and shouted obscenities assailed my ears and I wished I was back in the bush. My knees felt weak with reaction and the only redeeming feature was that I was relatively safe on the edge of the highway.

Table Mountain towered above me, its strangely flattened crest surprisingly free from cloud. I didn't dare push my luck any further by stopping for a photograph and I worked my way around the mountain with the rest of the commuters. At last I spotted a side road off the freeway, dashed into it and there was Cape Town spread out below me.

There it was, the city that I hadn't seen in over thirty years. The city that had been the focal point of my dreams and efforts for a very long time indeed. The sun was shining for once and it all looked peaceful and somehow unreal. A tanker lay at anchor in Table Bay and I felt tears well in my eyes at the thought that my journey was well and truly over. I had lived for this moment for so very long and now that it had arrived, all I could do was cry.

In the city itself, I treated myself to a celebratory cup of coffee and tried to look as though I cycle vast distances as a matter of course. I received a couple of curious glances, but Capetonians are accustomed to eccentric travellers and most of them barely spared me a glance. I asked directions to the Mount Nelson from a cheerful gentleman who welcomed me courteously to his city and once I had my destination pin-pointed, retired to the city gardens to wait for ten o'clock and my final grand entrance.

For half an hour I sat among the tall trees and beautifully tended flowerbeds. I savoured the scent of exotic blooms and enjoyed the frolicking squirrels and pretty girls of Cape Town. The sun was warm on my back and sunshine has a special quality in the Cape – probably because of its rarity. It seemed somehow more soothing and gentle than sunshine elsewhere in the world, but that was possibly due to my mood. For all my fears about arriving in that great city, I was suddenly content.

As the magic hour approached, my nervousness began anew. I kept jumping up from my bench to check Harriet over, even though I was three minutes from the Mount Nelson and nothing could possibly go wrong at that stage. The gear cable seemed to be held together by a single strand but it had been like that for ages and I could walk to the Mount Nelson if I had to. The tyres were solidly reassuring and suddenly there was no reason to delay any longer. Taking a deep breath to stifle wriggling butterflies, I wheeled Harriet out of the gardens and on to a road near Parliament Buildings. Climbing into the saddle, I pedalled toward my ultimate destination. I was going to arrive in style.

I had given myself exactly four minutes to reach the hotel gates but for the first time in seven and a half thousand kilometres, I managed to get myself lost.

I cycled round one corner, then another. The roads all looked the same. I asked a pedestrian. He didn't know. I asked a motorist at a set of traffic lights. He sent me back the way I had come. In a state of acute frustration, I eventually found my way back to the gardens and walked from there. Not quite as dignified perhaps but I was already ten minutes late and it seemed an infinitely safer way of getting to the Nellie.

With the ornate gates of the Mount Nelson in front of me at last, I whispered a prayer of thanks and remounted Harriet to cycle through in style. I might as well put a little pezazz into my arrival, even if it didn't seem as though there was anyone there to see it. The pith-helmeted security guard on duty threw me a salute and suddenly I felt a huge grin breaking out on my face. I felt wonderful. It didn't matter about the lack of a reception committee. I had made it. All on my own – well, with Harriet's help – I had done what I set out to do. My achievement would mean little to anyone else but it had been an experience I would never forget. Feeling like bursting into song – I might have for all I know – I cycled up the long, winding driveway that leads to the hotel itself.

My euphoria was enhanced and my contentment complete when the very first people I saw in the hotel grounds were Don and Maryanne Burton. They had delayed their own departure to welcome me in and I leaped off my bike to embrace them both. Tears ran down my cheeks and it was a wonderful moment. Even Don's rather gloomy greeting did nothing to dispel my elation.

"There's no sign of a reception committee," he said lugubriously but I didn't care. In fact it was a relief. I didn't want to meet the Press, although I did wonder what had happened to Frances Bond. She probably hadn't been able to make it and there was no way, she could have let me know. Shrugging all worries aside, I turned back to my friends.

"Never mind; let's go and get some coffee. Better still, how about a cold beer?"

With one arm around Maryanne's shoulders, the other supporting Harriet and my eyes bubbling with happy tears, I walked up to the hotel entrance, hardly noticing a slim lady who approached from a nearby car.

"Are you David Lemon?" She asked anxiously and I nodded in silent bemusement. She went on.

"We are from the Argus," she indicated a photographer who had appeared behind her. "Would you mind going back to the gate for a few photographs?"

"Only if my friends from Zambia can come with me," I told her and she agreed enthusiastically.

Walking back down the long drive with Don pushing Harriet and my arms around both ladies, I felt that my happiness had to be complete.

CHAPTER SIXTEEN

(Reflections)

It all seems a long time ago and my curtains are drawn against the bleak winter night as I write. Harriet rests in a shed outside and the kindly folk of Africa seem part of another world. In this cramped, English countryside, I find it difficult to think of my journey with Harriet as anything but a distant dream.

Nick Seewer and his team at the Mount Nelson were wonderful to me. They laid on a Champagne reception and put the entire hotel at my disposal. The suite – no mere bedroom for this hedonistic wanderer – I was given usually cost an absolute fortune and I horrified the little lady on dining room duty by turning up for dinner without a jacket. At the Nellie, that just was not done, but I was rescued by the Maitre d' and wasted no time in taking full advantage of the dazzling display of food on offer. Crayfish starters and underdone roast beef were a far cry from *nshima* and caterpillars I can assure you.

The Nellie was as luxuriously friendly as ever and I was only too happy to give Nick the 1963 invoice, wherein accommodation for six of us cost slightly less than morning tea for me when Harriet and I descended upon the place.

Frances Bond had not forgotten me. She was waiting in the foyer when I arrived and missed my grand entrance, as well as the champagne and photographs at the gate. She guided me through the subsequent interviews however and was a great help with all the trappings of luxurious domesticity that I was suddenly faced with.

Don and Maryanne Burton headed back to Zambia, while Harriet was whisked away by Pritchard Security for airfreight to Johannesburg and then back to England. I followed in due course, after spending time in joyful rest and recreation with my family in various parts of South Africa.

⌒⌒⌒

So it is all over and I am left with only my memories to sustain me through the English winter. What wonderful memories they are too. Outside, a vixen yammers into the night and I am back in Africa. My mind has fled the dank, Cotswold countryside and is back on dusty roads with distant horizons and laughingly hospitable people. I smell again the fragrance of mopani and frangipani in the sunshine. The call of the vixen becomes the eerie howl of foraging hyena and I am lost. My sleep will be restless again tonight and I shall hear again the sounds of hunters great and small, smell again the gritty dust of Masailand and see again the beaming smiles of welcome that are so much a part of Africa.

My journey from Nairobi to Cape Town took four months and fourteen days. During that time, Harriet and I covered seven thousand, three hundred and fifty-six kilometres. She suffered fifty-nine punctures and I lost seventeen kilograms in weight. Mind you, I ended up leaner, fitter and in better health than I had enjoyed in many a long year. Neither of us suffered any major damage and if my pride was dented or my dignity impaired on a couple of occasions, I ended up no worse for the experience.

As for Harriet – well, I thought she was in better shape than I was at the end, but that wasn't quite the case. When I finally took her back to Alan's cycle shop for a check up, he was aghast.

"What have you done?" He demanded, running his hands lovingly over my battered bicycle. I didn't know what he was going on about.

"Look at those front forks. They are so badly buckled, it is a surprise that you managed to move at all."

It could only have happened when I hit the Tanzanian pothole and even George Ugulumu hadn't noticed the deeper damage. Alan went on to assure me that I had been in imminent danger of having my bike collapse beneath me whenever I applied the brakes.

As Cape Town is a little over five and a half thousand kilometres beyond Kibidulla, Harriet hadn't done badly for a crippled machine. Mind you, I don't suppose I did much braking over those long, lonely roads. It always seemed such a waste of effort. Perhaps the *tokoloshe* really was looking after me.

I am often asked whether I would do the trip again. It is a question that was easy to answer in the weeks after it ended. Of course I would not. At the time, I was weary, my muscles were sore and my bottom had received enough saddle-battering to last it a lifetime.

Now I am not so sure. I sometimes talk to Harriet in her shed and we plan further adventures – other great escapes from the plastic nightmare of civilisation.

America perhaps – I have always wanted to visit the American West and Dan Butler's tales of Oregon further whetted my appetite. Canada, Australia, Europe or the Far East – all have their individual appeal but it is Africa that is still the focus of my dreams. It is Africa that holds my memories. Memories of friendly people, vast landscapes and incidents too numerous for inclusion in these pages. Memories of folk like Todi Siani who rode with me for fifty kilometres of rural Zambia. Incidents such as the time when – no perhaps I shouldn't go into that.

They are wonderful memories and will keep me going through the long dark winter. After that? Well, I don't suppose it will be too long before my beloved Harriet and I are heading once more for the most fascinating continent of them all.

Perhaps I can fit a small motor to her next time.

THE END

GLOSSARY

Anopheles	:	The genus to which malarial mosquitoes belong.
Biltong	:	The dried meat of Africa.
Boma	:	A protective thorny barrier protecting homestead or village.
Bonsela	:	Monetary tip or bribe.
Dagga	:	Cannabis or marijuana.
Duka	:	Small store, usually run by Indians.
Frikadelln	:	German rissoles or meatballs.
Fundi	:	Expert.
Hodi	:	Greeting – 'Is anyone home.'
Kali	:	Swahili word for 'cheeky.' Traditional beer in Botswana.
Kopje	:	Small rocky outcrop, often containing caves or tunnels.
Kraal	:	Rural African village.
Kwacha	:	Monetary unit of Zambia – value fluctuates.
Lekker	:	Afrikaans word for 'very nice' or 'super.'
Mandazi	:	A sugary batter cake, enjoyed throughout East Africa.
Manyatta	:	Masai village, also known as an 'engang.'
Ma-cranks	:	Colloquial expression meaning gears.
Marungu	:	White person south of the Zambezi.
Madhala	:	Respectful Chishona word for old man.
Masoda	:	Any fizzy drink.

Mealie	:	Corn on the cob.
Mealie meal	:	Stodgy maize porridge, known variously as mpufu, nshima, pap, pollichi, posho, sadza and ugali in the countries through which I passed.
Mombie	:	Chishona word for cow.
Moran	:	Masai Warrior – plural 'morani.'
Msasa	:	Deciduous tree.
Mtoto	:	Swahili word for child.
Muezzin	:	Muslim call to prayer.
Mzee	:	Swahili word for old man.
Mzungu	:	White person north of the Zambezi.
Nkosi Pezulu	:	God – literally, Lord Above.
Njinga	:	Colloquial word for bicycle.
Panga	:	African machete.
Paw paw	:	Papaya fruit.
Picannin	:	Southern African word for child.
Shuka	:	Red blanket garment worn by the Masai menfolk.
Swahili	:	Lingua Franca of East Africa.
Tokoloshe	:	Mischievous spirit of Southern Africa.
Tsotsi	:	Petty crook.
Veld	:	African bush countryside.
Voetsak	:	Derogative Afrikaans word for 'go away.'
Wazungu or Wzungu	:	White people – plural of Mzungu.

Printed in the United Kingdom by
Lightning Source UK Ltd., Milton Keynes
138978UK00001B/1/P